Капуста

Капуста

Kapusta
by
Erín Moure

a play-poem-ash,
a cabaret

"All ash is *pollen*."
Novalis

ANANSI

This edition published in 2015 by
House of Anansi Press Inc.
110 Spadina Avenue, Suite 801
Toronto, ON, M5V 2K4
Tel. 416-363-4343
Fax 416-363-1017
www.houseofanansi.com

Distributed in Canada by
HarperCollins Canada Ltd.
1995 Markham Road
Scarborough, ON, M1B 5M8
Toll-free tel. 1-800-387-0117

Distributed in the United States by
Publishers Group West
1700 Fourth Street
Berkeley, CA, 94710
Toll-free tel. 1-800-788-3123

House of Anansi Press is committed to protecting our natural
environment. As part of our efforts, the interior of this book is printed
on paper made from second-growth forests and is acid-free.

19 18 17 16 15   1 2 3 4 5

Library and Archives Canada Cataloguing in Publication
Mouré, Erin, 1955-, author
Kapusta / Erín Moure.
Poems.
Issued in print and electronic formats.
ISBN 978-1-77089-481-5 (pbk.).—ISBN 978-1-77089-482-2 (pdf)
ISBN 978-1-77089-983-4 (bound.)
I. Title.
PS8576.O96K36 2015   C811'.54   C2015-900526-4
C2015-900527-2

Library of Congress Control Number: 2014953280

Cover design and text design: Erín Moure
Typesetting: Brian Morgan

*We acknowledge for their financial support of our publishing program
the Canada Council for the Arts, the Ontario Arts Council, and the
Government of Canada through the Canada Book Fund.*

Canada Council   Conseil des Arts
for the Arts   du Canada

ONTARIO ARTS COUNCIL
CONSEIL DES ARTS DE L'ONTARIO
an Ontario government agency
un organisme du gouvernement de l'Ontario

Printed and bound in Canada

Капуста *Kapusta*

◆

*[At right: original text
At left: French text translated into English]*

◆

Upstage stage right, a wood-stove, assembled, with fire. Also upstage, six spindle-back kitchen chairs, a wooden table with leaves dropped. Doorway and door at stage right, an open doorway at stage left. Simple bench, centre, and a field of cabbages (real cabbages laid over a large brown canvas tarpaulin) beside the bench at stage left. The figurants are under the tarp in rows and real green cabbages are atop the canvas, in rows as in a field or cemetery. (The wood-stove is a construct of cardboard or plywood and hinges, so it collapses flat. To "light" it, glow rings are put on the burners and a log with a plywood flame in it is placed in the firebox.) **Only the cabbages are real.**

The poem unfolds in steps,
deploys in weavings, diffracts in sounds,
reflects in the golds of the room,
and refracts
from the silk of the stoles.

Jacques Rancière
Malaise dans l'esthétique

КАПУСТА

A play-poem-pollen

Principal actors:

E. woman in 40s or 50s, simply a vowel

MIM marionette 1-metre high, woman in her 40s with the easeful glamour of a young Jackie Kennedy pre-1963, before a shot

Fs figurants × 4. All races, heights, sexes, or any sex in between. They are villagers, stagehands, chorus, missives, or they simply crawled out of MIM's ear

U. usher, dressed as a trumpeter out of a cuckoo clock

Маленька Дочка Malenka Dotchka, *little daughter*, a sock-monkey in an apron, a vest, various hats

Note: MIM and Маленька Дочка are manipulated by figurants.

Family and locals:

2 ACTION DOLLS brothers

LEON OR old lion, plush, who calls herself *lioness* and *Orph,eu* and is the city Lviv, simply a dreamer

JAN EEYORE donkey of felt, simply what cannot be said

KAT vase or funerary urn from a dollar store, bearing a cat design, simply the frozen time of immigration (with cat allergy)

iPHONE plus a flashlight, mirror, fire, radio, piano, hat, veil, simply translators

CABBAGES heads or hyperbolic contingencies, simply real

Note: At times, actors read not just their lines, but the stage directions, and even the lines of others. They use as much French as the local audience can bear, but should at least use a few phrases. *"The language of the text is obsessional, and this must be faced."*

(Turn off your ideas)

U. Good evening, ladies and gentlemen. Please do not turn off your telephones, your pagers, your televisions, your radios, your PlayStations, your iPhones, your Androids, your agonized coughing, your digestive whimpers, your pustules, your circulatory systems, your cancers, your testicles, your uteruses, your spasms. Turn off your ideas!

ACT ONE: PARADISE
Scene 1 (Éteindre vos idées)

        USHER *enters downstage at centre.*

U. Bonsoir, mesdames et messieurs. Veuillez ne pas éteindre vos téléphones, vos téléavertisseurs, vos télévisions, vos radios, vos PlayStation, vos iPhone, vos Android, vos toux agonisantes, vos gargouillements digestifs, vos furoncles, vos systèmes de circulation sanguine, vos cancers, vos testicules, vos utérus, vos spasmes. Éteignez vos idées !

> *Figurants under the tarp sit up, disrupting the cabbages, then move everything offstage, starting with the tarp, stacking the cabbages meanwhile in a wheelbarrow and leaving them but taking the chairs, table, wood, doorways, bench, and collapsing the stove (leaving it). Finally one figurant comes out and removes the cabbages.*
>
> *The stage is bare.*
>
> *A phone rings in the public.*
>
> **E.** *gets up from the public, looks around, confused or perturbed, silent, partly lit up by her phone, and darts offstage. As she goes, she answers the phone and we hear her voice . . . she turns and faces the public at one point, taken aback by their presence.*

E. Tak, tak . . . yak spravy? dobre, dobre . . . tak . . . ne . . . ya ne znayu . . .

> **E.** *enters upstage, shuts off her phone, walks across stage, surveys, walks back, finds a cabbage leaf left behind, puts her phone down, picks up the leaf, curious, not facing the public, puts it on her head.*
>
> **F.** *enters and gives* **E.** *a woman's hat, stylish in a 1950s New York way, black with a short veil. Puts it on E.'s head*

adapted during the Hungarian Revolution in 1956 to express the homesickness of refugees, renamed "Honvágydal": ☐ *www.youtube.com/watch?v=1Trr1SpCg90*

over the cabbage leaf, bends to pick up the phone then exits.

E. *stands and goes to look at the collapsed stove in upstage right corner, and begins to build it again. While E. works, F. enters with a bench then exits after placing bench in centre.*

E. *finishes the stove and stands back, sees the bench and sits on it. Then she gets up, takes off the hat and leaf, looks around to decide where to put it. She sets it on the bench and sits again, beside it. She sings. As if in that great American art form, the musical.*

E. The first time we sang a song
     it was scar tissue
     The second time we sang
     it was joy
     Shall I sing it another time?
     Shall we sing the song again tomorrow?

     Be mine, be mine sang the radio box speaker
     sanguine

     I forget the song, I don't know the song
     Boots on, we're going (another memory like this)*
     Door's wide, we're gone

> **E.** *stands and pushes the bench behind the stove, takes the hat with cabbage leaf and puts it on a corner of the stove, then lies down on the bench behind the stove. The public sees only her head.*

E. There's a smell to the dirt when the season's about to change — I want to leave on a boat, the snow's gone, I want

---

* *to the tune of "Memories Are Made of This," a hit in 1956 — watch Dean Martin's eyes: ▢ www.youtube.com/watch?v=NS2k43NJycE*
adaptée pendant la révolution hongroise de 1956 pour exprimer le mal du pays des réfugiés ... renommée « Honvágydal » ▢ www.youtube.com/watch?v=1Trr1SpCg9o

to build a house, a leaf fell, I want to be a child, vernaculars deflect thought, and I lose sight of why. To make the act of knowing visible over time. The shapes give form to forms. And so the image becomes something else.

E. *sings, to the tune of* "O Little Town of Bethlehem."

```
The ears of hills are longer now
The limbs of trees are still
I don't know if love can grow
Or even if it will.

Oh light of all my rigamarole
Oh flower of my desire.
If I could be here one more day
You know I could go higher.

With bullets in their chambered guns
With wheat in all their bowls
I was born and I will die
But I will not grow old.

The young crawled through the boards at night
In Bibkra that year
They ate the pits of broken cherries
Then turned back round in fear.
```

She stops.

Speaks, as if reciting.

You could have played the piano on their backs, with sticks. Their vertebrae stuck out like xylophone keys.

Sings, a marching tune.

```
I came with an oath out of the garbage.
I came with a smile!
I came with a cabbage to win you over, after
a while.
```

(The impossible language)

E. She lets me rest here, behind the stove, even if my mother thinks it's too hot, thinks I'll burn myself or get an infection, have a heart attack at the age of five, or just catch a fever.

From here I can hear the voices of the others. Their conversations I don't understand. The old men who come into my grandmother's house and sit down on the chairs. Friends of my grandfather, immigrants now old. Who had worked hard in their lives. Who had seen things. Who had made decisions so their families could live.

The attention of my grandmother to these old men. No silence. Too much conversation. I don't get any of it. They speak the language that is neither English nor French. The language without name, impossible in Canada. My mother knows this impossible language.

My grandmother is rarely there, among the voices. She is close to the stove, her representative; she cooks. She makes bread, soups, meats, stuffed cabbage leaves.

My grandmother Anastasia. She's been dead for decades already. It's been over fifty years. And she died a second time eight years ago, when my mom left us. But she exists in me still. She is, my grandmother, not the memory of a caress, but the very fact of the caress. Is that possible?

F. comes out with a tiny toy piano. Sets it down centre downstage and exits. Lights dim.

ACT ONE, **Scene 2 (La langue impossible)**

> *E. speaks from behind the stove upstage. Lights. The toy piano is still downstage. The hat with the cabbage leaf now beside it.*

E. Elle me laisse reposer ici, derrière le poêle, même si ma mère pense que c'est trop chaud, que je risque de me brûler ou d'attraper une infection, de subir un infarctus à l'âge de 5 ans, ou tout simplement de déclencher une fièvre.

D'ici j'entends les voix des autres. Leurs conversations que je ne comprends pas. Les vieux qui entrent et s'assoient sur les chaises dans la maison de ma grand-mère. Les amis de mon grand-père, des immigrants maintenant vieux. Qui ont travaillé dans leurs vies. Qui ont vu des choses. Qui ont pris des décisions pour faire vivre leurs familles.

L'attention prêtée à ces vieux par ma grand-mère. Pas de silence. Trop de conversation. Je ne comprends rien. Ils parlent la langue qui n'est ni le français ni l'anglais. La langue sans nom. La langue impossible au Canada. Ma mère comprend cette langue impossible.

Ma grand-mère est rarement là, parmi les voix. Elle est près du poêle, son représentant ; elle cuisine. Elle fait le pain, les potages, les viandes, les feuilles de chou farcies.

Ma grand-mère Anastasie. Elle est morte depuis des décennies déjà. Depuis plus de cinquante ans. Et elle est morte une deuxième fois il y a huit ans, quand ma mère nous a quittés. Mais elle existe encore en moi. Elle est, ma grand-mère, non pas la mémoire d'une caresse, mais la caresse même. Est-ce possible ?

Her warmth has forever been with me. When life makes me anxious, I hear her voice. I feel the touch of her hand. I lie back down behind the stove in the kitchen of her house beside the creek.

But I can't go on forever, as my grandmother does. When I die, I will pass her caress, her voice, her proximity, and the responsibility for this caress, to you. Because I have no one else. Just you.

E.   Her house holds the aromas of cabbages and dill. Storm sensations. Borshcht. At the edge of a town in the north of Alberta, on the banks of Bear Creek, with the aspen poplars that still remain from the poplar wood, and with a field, a prairie nearby, the rich depth of the creek soil, close by. These days, no one lives by the creek like that, there are floods. But before, yes, there were houses.

Sa chaleur ne m'a jamais quittée. Quand la vie me trouble, j'entends sa voix. Je ressens sa caresse. Je me mets encore une fois derrière le poêle dans la cuisine de sa maison près du ruisseau.

Mais je ne pourrai continuer à tout jamais, comme ma grand-mère. Quand je mourrai, je vous passerai sa caresse, sa voix, sa proximité, la responsabilité de sa caresse. Car je n'ai personne d'autre. Je n'ai que vous.

> **F1** *enters and looks for* **E.**, *not seeing her at first. E. gets up, pretends she hadn't been sleeping at all. F1 hands E. the burner rings and the log with flame in it. E. "lights" the stove. F1 exits. While E. watches the stove,* **F2** *brings out the box of firewood, places it upstage then comes and looks at the stove with E.*

E.   *(to F2)* Didn't I have a cabbage leaf?

> **F2** *goes downstage to get the leaf from the hat and brings it to* **E.** *Hat remains by the toy piano.*

E.   Might I have a pot too? With water?

> **F3** *emerges with a pot and* **E.** *puts it on the stove with the cabbage leaf in it. F3 and* **F2** *exit.*

E.   *(stirs)* Sa maison garde le parfum des choux et de l'aneth. Sensations d'orage. Bortsch. Aux abords d'une petite ville du nord de l'Alberta, à côté du ruisseau Ours, avec les peupliers faux-trembles qui restent encore de la vieille tremblaie, et avec un champ, une prairie pas loin, son sol riche amené là par le ruisseau, tout près. Aujourd'hui, il n'y a personne qui vit près du ruisseau comme ça, il y a des inondations. Mais avant, oui, il y avait des maisons.

> **F1** *and* **F2** *enter with a model of the house and field and trees on a kind of stretcher and place it on the floor*

F1.   When I was small, the relation between things, their sizes, was all mixed up in my head. The world was small and insignificant, apart from the trees. But my grandmother's kitchen was big, bigger than a tree, bigger than a world. Everything can be found in my grandmother's kitchen. Everything is sheltered. All is safe. And so language can exist. Words.

And yet, I never understood any of the words that were pronounced in that kitchen. Hot. In the company of the caress.

F1.   Could you please take all this stuff away?

> **F2** *and* **F3** *carry everything offstage, house, piano, hat, all.*

F1.   I don't want to stay outside, with my brothers . . .

F1.   . . . I want to absorb the impossible voices and this strange language. Radio!

*downstage by the piano and hat. F1 places a lit phone in
it so the house illuminates the trees. F1 speaks.*

F1. Quand j'étais petite, la relation entre les choses, leurs tailles,
était toute mêlée dans ma tête. Le monde était petit et
insignifiant, sauf les arbres. Mais la cuisine de ma grand-
mère était grande, plus grande qu'un arbre, plus grande qu'un
monde. Dans la cuisine de ma grand-mère, tout se trouve.
Tout est à l'abri. Tout est protégé. Ainsi, le langage peut
exister. Des mots.

Pourtant, je n'ai rien compris des mots qui ont été prononcés
dans cette cuisine-là. Au chaud. En compagnie de la caresse.

*To **F2**, pointing to the model house.*

F1. Pourriez-vous enlever tout ça, s'il vous plait ?

F2 *et* **F3** *enlèvent tout, maison et piano, chapeau, tout.*

F1. Je ne veux pas rester dehors, avec mes frères ...

F4 *enters with* **2 action dolls** *and walks toward where
the house was, but it is too late, the model is gone, F4
stands still with the dolls.*

F1. ... je veux absorber les voix impossibles et cette langue
inconnue. Radio !

F3 *enters with a radio (simply a phone placed in a glass to
amplify sound from the internet) that speaks in Ukrainian
with the accent of Western Ukraine, and sets it downstage.
F3 exits, returns with a chair, hangs coat on the back, and
sits.* **All Fs** *come out with spindle-back chairs, jostle each
other, arrange chairs in a row, hang coats, sit against the
wall, talk.* **F4** *stands, holding the action dolls.*

E. How many times can I write this poem again?
    without knowing the alphabet
    the light in the glass of the window
    a grey day
    it's so grey

    Thinking of the massacres and of how they
    detached the skin
    from their arms, pulling it to the ground

    Held at distance
    I touched the place where your arm hit me
    Abscess of doubt
    Access corrupted
    or
    doubt

    My home is no longer here
    the leaves in long shards of glass on the trees
    it's the grass where I walk or heal

    Knife they took from me
    at the airport (unease)

E. Brothers! Go play outside! (*and to M.D.*) Go play outside with
    your brothers!

E. looks satisfied, the stage is populated; she goes back behind the stove and lies down. All the public sees is her head. **U.** *comes out holding* **Маленька Дочка** *and E. sings:*

E. Combien de fois puis-je écrire ce poème ?
    sans connaître l'alphabet
    la lumière à travers la vitre des fenêtres
    une journée grise
    c'est si gris

    Pensant aux massacres et comment ils ont
    détaché la peau
    de leurs bras, la tirant vers le sol

    Tenue à distance
    J'ai touché l'endroit où ton bras m'a frappée
    Abcès de doute
    Accès corrompu
    ou
    doute

    Ce n'est plus chez moi ici maintenant
    les feuilles en aiguilles de verre sur les arbres
    c'est l'herbe où je marche et où je guéris

    Couteau qu'ils m'ont pris
    à l'aéroport (malaise)

> *E. rises and approaches **F4** who still holds the brother dolls.*

E. Allez jouer dehors, les frères ! (*et à M.D.*) Va jouer dehors avec tes frères !

> *F. exits with dolls;* **U.** *exits leaving* **M.D.** *on the floor downstage, back to public. Radio silent in its glass near M.D. Other* **Fs** *stop talking.* **E.** *is lit. She sits on the centre chair.*

(Among the cabbages)

E.   In those days, paradise was already lost, we were happy in my grandmother's garden where we'd run down to the creek with its waters that spilled rivulets into the grass though those waters were forbidden us, so we played instead between the cabbages, between the peas climbing up stretched strings, but above all between the cabbages with their huge heads eaten by insects and worms, the fragrance of the garden was always the smell of those cabbages of my grandmother that held sun, heat, the languor of those days of summer.

E.   Among those cabbages, I knew paradise lost, I was two years old, I was five. Paradise doesn't last, lost paradise lasts but little.

The stage, that assemblage of particles, the body that constructs the stage by its presence, by its incorporation of presence as an equal! body and stage! body before stage! body constituted of rooms, upon a stage.

Anonymity of the murmur!

When I was eight years old, my grandmother died, the exact day JFK was shot in Dallas. My mother wasn't there near the garden with her dying mother, she was in the city with me and the radio that announced the shooting and we were there together gunned down in our living room, the day they announced the shooting of JFK, it's not every day all the

ACT ONE, Scene 3 (Parmi les choux)

> **E.** *still seated on centre chair. Other chairs gone.* **M.D.** *downstage centre, the radio-phone-glass.*

E.   Dans ce temps-là, le paradis était déjà perdu, nous étions heureux dans le jardin de ma grand-mère où nous courions vers le ruisseau avec ses eaux débordant à travers l'herbe, ces eaux qui nous avaient été défendus, alors on jouait entre les choux, entre les petits pois grimpant le long de fils tendus, mais surtout entre les choux avec leurs grandes têtes trouées d'insectes et de vers, l'odeur du jardin était toujours l'odeur de ces choux de ma grand-mère qui captaient le soleil, la chaleur, la lenteur de ces jours d'été.

> **E.** *stands. Indicates the cabbages.*

E.   Parmi ces choux j'ai connu le paradis perdu, j'avais deux ans, j'avais cinq ans. Le paradis ne dure pas, le paradis perdu dure peu.

La scène, cet assemblage de particules, et le corps qui construit la scène par sa présence, par son incorporation de la présence en tant qu'égale ! corps et scène ! corps devant scène ! corps constitué de pièces, à l'avant-scène.

L'anonymat du murmure !

> **2 Fs** *enter and quietly dismantle the stove behind* **E.**, *gesturing in a kind of pantomine at each other and at E., who is mesmerized by thought and does not see them.*

Quand j'avais huit ans, ma grand-mère est morte, le jour même de l'assassinat de JFK à Dallas. Ma mère n'était pas là près du jardin pour accompagner sa mère agonisante, elle était en ville avec moi et la radio qui annonçait l'assassinat et on était ensemble assassinées là dans notre salon, le jour de l'annonce de l'assassinat de JFK, ce n'est pas tous les jours que toutes les

radios in the world announce the same thing, and Dallas where we had never been is just one little point on the planet, like all the other little points, always little, but from that particular point, little as it was, the news came over the radio. A person shot dead is already shocking, and everywhere people heard the news on their radios, even in the USSR, even in Bibrka, Ukraine which still had its Russian Soviet name Bobrka, they probably listened to this news.

Only my grandmother did not receive the news of the assassination on November 22, 1963, she was dying without her daughter, who was with me, her daughter was my mother. I too am a daughter to my grandmother. Thus a sister to my mother: her big sister!

"You always preceded me," said my mother. "You were never littler than me."

    E. *pauses.*

My grandmother's death was not the end of caps and cabbages. My grandfather lived alone afterward and grew them on his own, alone. The same cabbages. Leaf upon leaf.

    E. *turns toward the stove, now dismantled.*

E. My grandmother was always in front of that stove. Her back to us, the hour hand of a clock, marking dinnertime. The moment that nourishes us. And now, in my heart, in the proximity of death, I feel her presence.

    F1 *and* **F2** *enter and place a huge tarp at stage left and then start to place the cabbages on top of it. F2 speaks.*

F2. The grandmothers took the little ones into their arms so that the mothers could live!

F1.   You can't sing here! It's a cemetery, it's not a synagogue!

radios du monde annoncent la même chose, et Dallas où on n'est jamais allées, rien qu'un tout petit point sur la planète, comme tous les autres petits points, toujours petits, mais de cet endroit même petit, c'est de là que nous venait la nouvelle à la radio. Une personne assassinée, c'est déjà choquant, partout on a entendu cette nouvelle à la radio, même en URSS, même à Bibrka en Ukraine qui portait encore son nom russe soviétique Bobrka, là aussi ils ont probablement écouté cette nouvelle.

Seule ma grand-mère n'a pas reçu cette annonce d'assassinat le 22 novembre 1963, elle était en train de mourir dans l'absence de sa fille, qui était avec moi, et cette fille, c'était ma mère. Moi aussi, je suis fille de ma grand-mère. Donc sœur de ma mère . . . sa sœur ainée !

« Tu m'as toujours précédée », disait ma mère. « Tu n'as jamais été plus petite que moi. »

> **E.** *pause.*

La mort de ma grand-mère n'était pas la fin ni des choses ni des choux. Mon grand-père a vécu seul après et les a cultivés, à lui seul. Les choux de toujours. Feuille sur feuille.

> **E.** *se tourne vers le poêle, maintenant démantelé.*

E. Ma grand-mère, elle était toujours devant ce poêle. Elle était debout, de dos, une aiguille d'horloge marquant l'heure du repas. L'heure qui nous nourrit. Et maintenant, dans mon cœur, dans la proximité de la mort, je la ressens.

> **F1** *et* **F2** *entrent et mettent une grande bâche sur le sol, côté cour, puis commencent à placer des choux là-dessus.* F2 *parle.*

F2. Les grands-mères ont pris les petits dans leurs bras afin que les mères puissent vivre !

F1. *(screaming in F2's face)* Ça ne chante pas ici ! C'est un cimetière, pas une synagogue !

E.   Yes, a cemetery. My grandparents didn't sing beside the
     Alberta creek where they lived in retirement, safe and sound,
     having emigrated before the war from their country of
     Ukraine, or Poland, or Austria. Only the creek sang, the aspens
     sang, the grey or blue sky didn't sing, human beings never
     sang, there was no human song. Food, yes, warmth, yes,
     people speaking to each other, their whispers that were
     foreign to me, yes . . . And my mother fled from all that so
     she could sing. She wanted to sing.

     Yes, to sing! To sing in a Canadian city in an urban Canadian
     house with Dean Martin on the television, Dean Martin
     boyfriend of my mother with his martini and banter, cracking
     jokes and yes, in our living room in Calgary in the evening,
     there was singing. *Everybody loves somebody, sometime*, we
     belted out . . .

                                            She seems to address M.D.

E.   My father told us, we're Spanish.

     No, no, my mother said to my father, half-Spanish! We're also
     Ukrainian. Or, if we're Spanish, I'm out of the picture. I'm not
     one of you. I'm from the Old Country!

     That's why all origin seemed to us a lie, a hoax, nothing but
     a bunch of hype. But how can the truth be spoken, except
     through fictions and lies? My mother and Dean Martin, lies!
     Dean Martin with his martini glass, crooning for women,
     fiction! To really be Canadian you had to be in love with a
     star on television, you had to sing! Who needs words or
     cemeteries; no! you have to sing!

*E. turns toward them. Is startled and stops, listens to **F1**. She
steps away from the dismantled stove. Turns back to look at
it. Light comes up on **Маленька Дочка** downstage
facing the public. Softer light on the field where F1 and **F2**
finish spacing out the cabbages. In a quiet voice in the dark
near the stove dissembly, E. speaks as if to herself.*

E.   Oui, un cimetière. Mes grands-parents ne chantaient pas à côté
du ruisseau albertain où ils vivaient retraités, sains et saufs,
après avoir émigré, avant la guerre, de leur pays l'Ukraine — ou
la Pologne, ou l'Autriche. Seul le ruisseau chantait, les faux-
trembles chantaient, le ciel gris ou bleu ne chantait pas, les êtres
humains ne chantaient pas, il n'y avait pas de chant humain. De
quoi manger, oui, de la chaleur, oui, des êtres parlant entre eux,
leurs murmures qui m'étaient étranges, oui . . . Et ma mère s'est
enfuie de tout ça afin de chanter. Elle voulait chanter.

Chanter, oui ! Chanter dans une ville canadienne dans une
maison urbaine canadienne avec Dean Martin à la télévision,
Dean-Martin-*boyfriend*-de-ma-mère avec son martini et sa
légèreté, toujours à faire des blagues et oui, dans notre salon
le soir à Calgary, ça chantait. *Everybody loves somebody, sometime,*
ça chantait . . .

       E. *steps downstage into* **M.D.**'s *light. Elle paraît parler à M.D.*

E.   Mon père nous disait, on est d'origine espagnole.

Non, non, ma mère disait à mon père, qu'en partie espagnole !
On est aussi Ukrainiens. Ou, si on est Espagnols, je ne le suis
pas. Je ne suis pas comme vous. Je suis du Vieux Pays !

Ainsi toute origine nous paraissait mensonge, tromperie,
fable. Mais comment alors manifester la vérité sinon à travers
la fiction et le mensonge ? Ma mère et Dean Martin, mensonge !
Dean Martin avec son verre de martini chantant pour les
femmes, fiction ! Pour vraiment être canadien, il fallait être
amoureuse d'une vedette de télévision, il fallait chanter ! Il ne
faut ni mots ni cimetières, non, non, il faut chanter !

Followed by a song
sung by the **Fs** *offstage.* 🔊

Fs. Imbecile!
Imbecile!
The writer of this play is
an imbecile!

In the hallway of shoes, the women's party shoes
are leaving! through their display windows!
Off they go!
Gone, gone, gone to earth!

In the hallway of shoes, the mirrors!
Are going, have flown, have blown.
Imbecile, imbecile, *scram*, what an imbecile!

All that will be left of you is . . . suitcases.
Words sewn into their handles. The tags of
suitcases are your books. Your names.

> **Fs** *enter and with brusque movements (nearly pantomine),*
> *they rebuild the stove and light it.*

E. Perhaps I cook today in Montreal, in Paris, in Kelowna, in Edmonton, thanks to my grandmother, perhaps I feel the heat of life in my own body, thanks to my grandmother who had always looked at me with a look I could not understand, of silence, of love, of the loss of paradise, of here.

Here!

Simply here.

We come from here. From nowhere.

Fs. From paradise.

*Light on **M.D.** downstage. **E.** bends down and turns on the radio, which plays M.D.'s **song #1**. Suivi d'une chanson chantée par des **F.** depuis les coulisses.* 🔊

Fs. Débile !
Débile !
L'écrivaine de cette pièce
est une débile !

Dans le corridor à souliers, les souliers de gala
des femmes sont en train de partir ! à travers
leurs vitrines ! Ils s'en vont !
Partir, partir. Par terre !

Dans le corridor à souliers, les miroirs !
S'en vont, sont envolés, sont vents.
Débile, débile, *décampez*, vous êtes débile !

Il ne restera de vous que . . . des valises. Des
mots cousus dans les poignées de ces valises. Les
étiquettes des valises sont vos livres. Vos noms.

> *Des **Fs** entrent et brusquement (presque de façon pantomime) reconstruisent le poêle et l'allument. **E.** lies on the bench behind it.*

E. Peut-être que je cuisine aujourd'hui à Montréal, à Paris, à Kelowna, à Edmonton, grâce à ma grand-mère, peut-être que je ressens la chaleur de la vie à même mon corps grâce à ma grand-mère, qui m'a toujours regardée avec un regard de je ne sais quoi, de silence, d'amour, de perte, de paradis, d'ici.

Ici !

Simplement ici.

On vient d'ici. De nulle part.

Fs. Du paradis.

(Salt-shaker love)

MIM.   Malenka Dotchka! Malenka Dotchka! I'm leaving you a note
under the salt shaker because I love you!

> **Four Fs** *enter with the dining table and the wooden chairs
> and set the table downstage centre beside the cabbage field.
> Light on them. None on* **M.D.**

F₁.   They say there were letters during the war, sent to Alberta.
Letters from the village, over there in the Old Country amid
the borders, yes, amid, for this border was wide, 200 kilometres
thick.

F₂.   That's how they knew everything! On their berry mountain
in Alberta. It was in the letters. There, it was all written.
Those who set these words on airmail paper lived all along
the railway that crossed the village on its way to Lvov-Lviv,
and then to Bełżec. Thus in Alberta, on the mountain, they
read those missives and knew everything; those immigrants
who laboured on the soils that once belonged to the Dane-zaa
knew everything in the bush and in the cold on the berry
mountain during that war.

ACT TWO: PTOLEMY
Scene 1 (Salière-amour)

> *Lights up on* **Маленька Дочка** *centre downstage, back
> to public. Hook and chair gone. Tarp and cabbages still
> there. Silence. Voice of* **MIM** *offstage.*

MIM. Malenka Dotchka ! Malenka Dotchka ! Je te laisse une note
sous la salière car je t'aime !

> **F.** *enters with salt shaker and note and places note under
> salt shaker beside* **M.D.** *who is lit but does not move, of
> course. M.D., strictly speaking, does not speak.*

> **F2** *enters upstage with* **MIM**, *a marionette dressed
> crisply for work as a nurse, cap included. MIM walks
> across stage in front of the stove (no E. behind) and both
> exit. Light on* **M.D.**, *salt shaker, and note. M.D. does not
> move, of course.*

> **Quatre Fs** *entrent ensemble avec la table et ses chaises
> et dressent la table au centre, à côté du champ de choux.
> Lumière sur eux. Rien sur* **M.D.**

F1. On dit qu'il y avait des lettres durant la guerre, envoyées en
Alberta. Des lettres du village, là-bas dans le Vieux Pays au
milieu des frontières, oui, au milieu, car cette frontière était
large de 200 kilomètres.

F2. Ainsi ils savaient tout ! Depuis leur montagne à petits fruits
en Alberta. Grâce aux lettres. Tout y était écrit. Ceux et celles
qui avaient consacré ces mots sur papier aérien habitaient
tout le long du chemin de fer qui traversait le village vers
Lvov-Lviv et après à Bełżec. Ainsi, depuis la montagne en
Alberta, en lisant ces missives, ils savaient tout ; ces immigrants
qui labouraient les anciennes terres des Dane-zaa, ils savaient
tout depuis la forêt et le froid de la montagne à petits fruits
pendant cette guerre.

F1. By reading those letters, yes. In them they heard the human song. MIM said this more than once to her daughter. But only the memory of the letters is left to us. We can no longer rely on letters! It's a nightmare to never again receive a letter. When there are no more letters, people forget! Those missives in two alphabets, alphabets of that village, Ukrainian and Polish. All that happened along the soldiers' road, beside their house! All that occurred along the little river, along the railway track! And on the little hill where her mother's parents lived, where she, MIM, had learned to stand up on her tiny feet near the little knoll. Malenka Dotchka's mother learned to walk there! In 1925, before she knew how to remember! Her first images were of the dining room of the liner that brought them to Liverpool, to Halifax. The tiny tables for the smallest children, 1929.

F4. So none of us were there during the war; we were anywhere but there, we were emigrants, we had our fields to till, we couldn't bear it anymore, it was no longer our country. It was our people, but they lived nowhere, their country had no name, had no place. The Old Country. For decades, this country had no name of its own, only the names imposed on it, Austro-Hungary, Poland, Galicia, Soviet Republic. We never spoke its name. Its name was abolished.   Nowhere, said MIM to her daughter; we know it because Malenka Dotchka is her daughter and it was her daughter to whom MIM said that she came from nowhere. The daughter could go live nowhere too; to get there, she lay down behind her grandmother's stove, like peasants in time of famine when everyone has lain down in their beds, so as to die or not die of hunger.

F3. But here, we see a different creek. We eat. We're grown up. We can talk. Nowhere is somewhere else. Here is here! There is no human song.

F₁.   Grâce à ces lettres, oui. C'était ça, le chant humain. MIM l'a dit plus d'une fois à sa fille. Mais seule la mémoire des lettres nous reste. On ne peut plus se fier aux lettres ! C'est un cauchemar de ne plus recevoir de lettres. Quand il n'y a plus de lettres, les gens oublient ! Ces missives aux deux alphabets, aux alphabets de ce village, ukrainien et polonais. Tout ce qui s'est passé le long du chemin des soldats, à côté de leur maison ! Tout ce qui est arrivé le long de la petite rivière, le long du chemin de fer ! Et sur la petite côte où habitaient les parents de sa mère, et où MIM a appris à se tenir debout sur ses pattes près de la petite colline. La mère de Malenka Dotchka a appris à marcher là-bas ! En 1925, avant de pouvoir en retenir le souvenir ! Ses premières images étaient de la salle à manger du paquebot qui les amenait à Liverpool, à Halifax. De très petites tables pour les plus petits enfants, 1929.

F₄.   Alors personne d'entre nous n'était là pendant la guerre … on était partout sauf là, on était des émigrants, on avait nos sols à labourer, on n'en pouvait plus, ce n'était plus notre pays. C'était nos gens, mais ils ne vivaient nulle part, leur pays n'avait ni de nom ni de lieu. Le Vieux Pays. Durant des décennies, ce pays n'a pas eu de nom à lui, que des noms imposés : Empire austro-hongrois, Pologne, Galicie, République soviétique. On ne disait plus son nom. Son nom avait été aboli. *Old Country.* Nulle part, disait MIM à sa fille ; on le sait, car Malenka Dotchka est sa fille, et à sa fille MIM disait qu'elle venait de nulle part. La fille elle aussi pouvait aller vivre nulle part ; pour y arriver, elle se couchait derrière le poêle de sa grand-mère, comme le faisaient les paysans en période de famine quand tout le monde se couchait dans son lit, pour mourir ou ne pas mourir de faim.

F₃.   Mais ici, on voit un autre ruisseau. On mange. On est grands. On peut parler. Nulle part, c'est ailleurs. Ici, c'est ici ! Il n'y a plus de chant humain.

> *Lights dim on **Fs** as they work. Lights up on **M.D.** and the salt shaker and note. Fs stop, turn in shadow toward the salt shaker.*

Fs. (*admiring voices*) Look at the salt shaker! There it is! Ah! (*an* **F.** *softly*) Malenka Dotchka was so well loved! Her mother left her a note and money to buy food, for her and for her brothers!

(Pericómo)

> **E.** *before the stove, cooking, the table all set nearby. She sings . . . her song becomes more and more slow, curious or perturbed, while she stares at the table. . . .*

E. Rustling river
    iron road
    that sings along
    that sings of wrong
    far-fetched
    butterfly above
    cold water mother of iron
    water what a   woe
    no water runs
    the . . . people — arrive . . . their . . .
        place . . . is gone

I listen to you, without wanting to enter the memories, contained in those letters now gone forever. There's no memory now. I grew up without memory! I had to fabricate myself out of nothing! Out of solitude and ashes.

> **F.** *enters with the marionette* **MIM** *still in nurse's uniform and stops in front of* **E.**

E. Courage, Mom!

MIM. (*moves without speaking, an awkward dance on the stage, almost in one place*)

E. (*perturbed*) Shut up!

Fs. (*voix heureuses*) Regardez la salière ! C'est là-bas ! Ah ! (*un* **F.** *à voix douce*) Malenka Dotchka a été tant aimée ! Sa mère lui a laissé une note et de l'argent pour acheter de quoi manger, pour elle et pour ses frères !

ACT TWO, Scene 2 (Pericómo)

> **E.** *devant le poêle en train de cuisiner, la table toute prête près d'elle. Elle chante . . . son chant devient de plus en plus lent, curieux ou perturbé, pendant qu'elle regarde la table. . . .*

E. Ruisseau, ruisseau
    chemin de fer
    de champ de faire
    de chant d'affaire
    farfelu
    papillon dessus
    fer mère l'eau froide
    l'eau oh oh ö
    pas d'eau ruisseau
    les . . . gens — arrivent . . . leur . . .
        place . . . est vide

Je vous écoute, sans vouloir pénétrer les souvenirs, contenus dans ces lettres déjà et pour toujours disparues. Comme ça, il n'y a plus de mémoire. J'ai grandi sans mémoire ! J'ai dû me fabriquer à partir de rien ! À partir de la solitude et des cendres.

> **F.** *entre sur scène avec la marionnette* **MIM** *toujours en tenue d'infirmière et arrête devant* **E.**

E. Courage, Maman !

MIM. (*bouge sans rien dire, une danse maladroite sur scène, presque sur place*)

E. (*perturbée*) Tais-toi !

E.   We should both shut up!

> *Silence. Dance stops.* **E.** *tries to hug the marionette, takes a step forward, but the marionette steps backward.*

E.   (*steps back . . . space, space . . .*) WORD!

> *Silence, then . . .*

MIM.   (*calm voice*) That's not shutting up!

> *Silence, then . . .*

You just shut up the content . . . STINKWORD!

E/   WORD!
MIM.

E.   COURAGE!

MIM.   From work well done, time is won! Do your homework!

> *Silence . . . no movement onstage.*

E.   (*calm voice*) If you are really my mother, you can sing . . . well, you can sing, oh . . . oh, oh . . . (*hesitates, excited, then serious*) Perry Como.

Pericómo! Paree-comb-oh . . . . . (singing) . . .

> *Another* **F.** *comes onstage with the radio . . . sounds emerge from it . . .*

E. Taisons-nous !

*Silence. La danse finit. **E.** tente d'embrasser la marionnette, fait un pas en avant, la marionnette recule.*

E. *(recule . . . espace, espace . . .)* VERBE !

Silence, puis . . .

MIM. *(voix tranquille)* Ce n'est pas se taire, ça !

Silence, puis . . .

Tu tais seulement le contenu . . . MALVERBE !

E/ VERBE !
MIM.

E. COURAGE !

MIM. D'un travail bien fait, le temps est né ! Fais tes devoirs !

Silence . . . pas de mouvement sur scène.

E. *(voix calme)* Si tu es vraiment ma mère, tu peux chanter . . . bon, tu peux chanter, bon . . . bon, bon. . . . *(hésite, excitée, puis sérieuse)* Perry Como.

Pericómo ! Paris-comme-oh . . . . . (chantant) . . . "dancing by the side of a stream". . .

*Un autre **F.** arrive sur scène avec la radio ; des sons en émergent. ▢ www.youtube.com/watch?v=kdK1wvKAFfg "Catch a falling star, and put it in your pocket, never let it get away . . . " (1957) with sound garbled and totally unlike the real song if necessary to avoid copyright problems.*

***MIM** is turned toward the radio, and dances without **E.** Who stands and watches. Suddenly MIM stops. **F.** looks*

(earth weigh lightly)

at MIM. E. watches her. MIM speaks, shaking her head sideways.

MIM.   Something is trying to crawl out of my ear!

MIM's *voice now rises from the* **radio**, *as if it is what is trying to crawl out of her ear:*

Space it out! What are you going to do with all that time? Days, hours, minutes! Not to mention hundreds of months. Decades! You've got decades ahead of you. Think! So you finish ten minutes early — what use is that? You're making me quite dizzy. One thing after another. Not so fast! And where's it going to end? What a waste of time! Dotchka, I shudder when I think that the earth takes a whole day to rotate. Yes, the twinkling of an eye! It's not eternity at all, it's the twinkling of an eye. That's quite clear. But then again, eternity is eternity is eternity.

Food for thought, Dotchka, food for thought! When I think about eternity I start worrying about the world.[1]

ACT TWO, Scene 3 (**terre légère**)

E. *lies behind stove, asleep. Downstage, table still set for 6. Four* **Fs** *enter, with* **U.**, *bringing* **MIM** *in dress clothes and hat, along with* **M.D.**, **L.O.**, **Jan Eeyore**, **Kat**. *Fs sit, animals on their laps as if lion, donkey, vase, MIM, and M.D. are family or guests who eat and converse, except: M.D. is set in a chair on her own and U. holds not a creature but the small radio-glass. The Fs/U. give voice to their creatures. M.D., strictly speaking, does not speak. Instead, the script is in front of her, and when someone*

---

1 *Any resemblance between what pours out of MIM's ear and the first lines of Büchner's* Woyzeck *played backwards is coincidental.*

M.D. (*to her brothers*) Quick, hurry! Let's go to the store and buy some day-old bread. It's still fresh and it's half price!

"if we start putting up monuments, we'll have to put them everywhere . . . all Ukraine is a cemetery"

"may the earth press lightly on us! on the men, on the women, on the children!"

"when you emerge from the bath all clean, you're fresh as a cabbage!"

wants to hear her, they grab it and read on her behalf,
shouting.

The small house is on the table. **Any one F.**/*animal says*
the following, with **M.D.**'s *words marked. It is as if* **E.** *is*
dreaming a cabaret of fitful language.

ANY: "But the bush firing trenches"

"It was necessary to put an end to consciousness."

"A monument of cement in the forest."

"the grave robbers!"

M.D. (*à ses frères*) Vite, vite ! on va aller acheter le pain d'hier. C'est
encore frais et c'est à moitié prix !

ANY: « si on commence à installer des monuments, il en faudra
partout ... toute l'Ukraine est un cimetière »

« que la terre soit légère sur nous ! sur eux, sur elles, sur les
enfants ! »

M.D. A sock monkey is a-temporal. A sock monkey stands between
the *Holocaust by Bullets* in Bibrka Ukraine and her mother the
nurse MIM who dresses like Jackie K.

ANY: « quand tu émerges de l'eau toute propre, tu es fraîche comme
un chou ! »

M.D. A sock monkey stands between her mother and the voice of
Perry Como. The sock monkey's clothes are backwards, and
her back is her face, her shoulder is her face. The sock monkey
is an онука, but her name is Маленька Дочка. The first song
she remembers is "Catch a Falling Star" by Perry Como, #1 in
Billboard, 1957. The sock monkey's face, "strictly speaking,
does not speak."

> **Fs** *in shared voices, abrupt now, interrupting each other.*
> *Their voices are the slap of cards in a game of chance.*
> *They've forgotten their creatures. . . .*

Thunder! Episteme! Hedge! Varnish!

Slide trombone game tallow!! Gallows giblets! Rapscallion! пройдисвіт!

Hedge-varnish! Thunder-capitalism!
Ectoplasm! Чудовисько Версальський!   *Operation Reinhard!*

ANY: They put on their socks / and ran away,
Large numbers, he said, are living in the woods in freezing
fate. Even old people shelter /
not spared. Young people in the wood
had run away from
hardened police and hidden fast in woods.
Tonnerre ! Epistème ! Buisson ! Vernis !
Sometimes troops fired on peasants as / they fled into the
woods. Women for some time / the inhabitants, on
hearing troops approaching, fled, an entire village into woods.
And found in hiding they tore off his pants and shirt. One
soldier sat on his neck, another crushed his legs, and / four
started to flay him. One child who was wounded by splinters of
/ wood
after the explosion another / unexploded / bomb was found at
They put on their boots and ran / away.
Graisse de trombone à coulisse ! Gibier de potence ! Gamin !
Water leaked into their boots, soaking the socks.
Bring boots on the stage and fill them with water. Put wooden
fishes into the boots. Pull socks out of the boots. Kick the boots
over. Get out of here ...
Buisson-vernis ! Tonnerre-capital ! Four-powers pact!
Ectoplasme ! Monstrosity of Versailles! Potsdam! *Einsatz
Reinhardt!*

> **Fs** *rise and exit in a clamour with the animals, knocking
> over chairs, leaving the radio and* **M.D.** *One* **F.** *re-enters
> and skids to a stop at the table, grabs and throws M.D.
> downstage, spluttering, indignant:*

F.   I am tired of the diarrhea rhetoric, OK! you cast it off and it
lands again as demagogy in embroidered shirts. No one wants
my memorial pain, OK! Caught between two enemas and a
friend, the library where all the zombies I had unearthed had
given way but other perverts of delirium still emerge. When
I think of memory, OK! I break its head. Bow to the pop
songsters, OK! Like me on Facebook! Pop pills! I don't know

E.   Granddaughter! Granddaughter!

(the grapefruits)

U.   Ladiesandgerms! How are your ideas now? Right now! An old
     plush lion (lights) (scene) (stage) (factory) roars only: "origin"
     "origin" to which sweet MIM marionette responds: imagine /
     gossip / far away. Our lion, Leon Orpheu, formerly a factory
     worker, now unemployed, symbol of Lviv, and poet who
     looked back. He enters; look at that carpenter apron! But he
     says he's Lioness now and not Lion, and she wishes a comma,
     please: *Leonne Orph,eu.*

               Leonne Orph,eu *enters in a carpenter's apron, borne
               by an* **F.** *who exits after placing her next to* **Маленька**

why I was fried, OK! by paranoids playing pinball with their blemish trollops. Undigested blurbs of redigerate vomiting and arguments, OK! What use are arguments to those who sacrificed for their country when a country is a palimpsest *merde* on *merde*. I am going to die from my face, OK! And bleat from an orifice! I am going to die from my arm, OK! and from my jointed elbow and I am going to die from my facial skin. I can't die from what's beneath, not from bone ground into cinders, not from squirming earth, OK! And I won't die from your festoon neuralgia.

> **E.** *wakes from her dream, rises from behind the stove and runs jagged to pick up* **Маленька Дочка**, *who has been left lying face down, her back (which is also her face) to the crowd. There is a large flash of white light and the radio rings like a telephone on the table. E. turns to call out, startled:*

F.   Онука! онука!

ACT TWO, Scene 4 (les pamplemousses)

> **U.** *enters alone, strutting like a trumpeter out of a cuckoo clock.*

U.   Mesdammessieurs ! Comment vont vos idées, alors ? Maintenant ! Un vieux lion en peluche (lumière) (scène) (planches) (usine) rugit seulement : « origine » « origine » auquel répond la douce MIM marionnette : devine / bavarde / lointain. Notre lion, Leon Orpheu, anciennement travailleur d'usine, aujourd'hui désœuvré, symbole de Lviv, et poète qui a regardé derrière lui. Il entre; regardez ce tablier de menuisier ! Mais il se veut Lionne dès lors, non pas Lion, et elle veut une virgule : *Lionne Orph,eu.*

> **Lionne Orph,eu** *en tablier de menuisier entre portée par un* **F.** *qui sort après l'avoir placée près de* **Маленька**

Дочка. *Voice of L.O. offstage, and a laser light pointed by another* **F.** *indicates a spot in the field when Leonne speaks; the light serves as her arm.* **U.** *speaks for our dear L.O. as her light points to the field and upturned chairs . . . in reality the lioness just lies motionless on the stage, as any plush toy or poet would do in a time of famine . . .*

L .   here's where we want to grow the flowers.

> **F.** *enters and stays in the shadow, speaks for* **M.D.** *who strictly speaking does not speak. M.D. remains immobile on the stage.*

M.D.   the grapefruits?

L.   gosh nooooo
grapefruits are fruits not flowers
grapefruits won't grow here anyhow

M.D.   but they will!

L.   well in Florida . . . we're not florid here

M.D.   well with flowers it's florid, and freely flourishes!

L.   notasinglegrapefruit!

> **F.** *and* **U.** *head offstage, bearing the table, the radio on it.*
>
> **E.** *enters, anxious, shadowy. She strides here and there. Finally she finds what she is looking for. She gathers up the sock monkey and gives* **Leonne Orph,eu** *a big kick. She murmurs, mocking . . .*

E.   Monkeys have always been oppressed by lions . . .
And the lion roars: origin! origin!
See what I mean? oppressed by lions.
But this is no lion! (it's a stuffed toy) . . .
Lion sheep monkey, I don't care . . . get out of my way!

Дочка. *Voix de L.O. en off, et un* **autre F.** *pointe un laser indiquant le champ tandis que Lionne parle ; cette lumière lui sert de bras.* **U.** *parle pour notre chère L.O. pendant que sa lumière pointe vers le champ et les chaises renversées . . . en réalité elle reste immobile sur les planches, comme n'importe quelle peluche ou poète le ferait en période de famine . . .*

L. voilà où on veut faire pousser des fleurs.

F. entre, reste à l'ombre et parle pour **M.D.** *qui, à strictement parler, ne parle pas. M.D. reste immobile sur les planches.*

M.D. des pamplemousses ?

L. non mais
les pamplemousses ne sont pas des fleurs
les pamplemousses de plus ne poussent pas ici

M.D. mais si !

L. mais en Floride . . . ici ce n'est pas floride

M.D. mais avec les fleurs c'est floride, ça fleurit !

L. pasdepamplemousse !

F. et U. sortent avec la table, la radio dessus.

E. entre, anxieuse, ténébreuse. Elle marche ici et là. Finalement elle trouve ce qu'elle cherche. Elle ramasse la poupée-singe et donne un gros coup de pied à **Lionne Orph,eu**. *Elle murmure, voix moqueuse . . .*

E. Les singes ont toujours été opprimés par les lions . . .
Et le lion rugit : origine ! origine !
Mais tu vois ? opprimés par les lions.
Mais ce n'est pas un lion ! (c'est une peluche)
Lion mouton singe, m'en fiche . . . dégage-moi le chemin !

Silence . . . then more gently, as if realizing . . .

But there are all sorts of ethnicities here . . .
We can even guess who is who (*indicates the chairs*) . . .

We don't want any songs of origin origin, get out, lioness! get out of here, monkey!

> **E.** *throws* **Leonne Orph,eu** *and* **M.D.** *offstage then looks at the field of cabbages. M.D. arrives again onstage, between E. and the public, in a stroller hurled from offstage, without any F.*

E.   (*imitates the monkey's voice, exaggerating*) stay away from me! i had a lousy sleep. i had my nightmares. grandma grandpapa!

(*in her own voice*) But, nightmares, really . . .

(*in the voice of M.D.*) my nightmares . . .

E.   (*in her own voice*) Your nightmares

(*in the voice of M.D.*) of fields of grain of fields of cabbage of grapefruitsssss.

(*in her voice, pushing the stroller*) Right here? For real?

> **F.** *emerges from the shadows behind* **M.D.** *and gives voice to her.*

M.D.   she wanted to plant flowers, the lioness did, and me i wanted grapefruits

E.   (*calm voice*) They don't grow here, grapefruits.

M.D.   such green grandeur those grapely fruits

E.   You make no sense, dear monkey.

M.D.   i'm no monkey, i'm the daughter of MIM, i am Malenka Dotchka

Silence . . . puis plus doucement, quasi émerveillée . . .

Il y a toutes sortes d'ethnies ici . . .
On peut deviner même qui est qui *(indique les chaises)* . . .

On ne veut pas de chants d'origine-origine, va-t'en lionne !
va-t'en singe !

> **E.** *lance* **Lionne Orph,eu** *et* **M.D.** *dans les coulisses.*
> *Après, elle regarde le champ de choux. M.D. arrive sur scène*
> *entre E. et le public dans une poussette jetée depuis les*
> *coulisses, sans F.*

E. *(imite la voix du singe, exagérée)* ne t'approche pas ! je n'ai pas
bien dormi. j'ai mes cauchemars. grand-mère grand-père !

(avec sa propre voix) Mais voyons, des cauchemars . . .

(avec la voix de M.D.) mes cauchemars . . .

E. *(avec sa propre voix)* Tes cauchemars

(avec la voix de M.D.) de champ de blés de champ de choux de
pamplemou . . . sses.

(avec sa voix, en poussant la poussette) Ici icitte ? Pour vrai ?

> **F.** *émerge de l'ombre derrière* **M.D.**, *et parle dans la*
> *voix de M.D.*

M.D. elle voulait planter des fleurs, la lionne, et moi des
pamplemousses

E. *(voix détendue)* Ça ne pousse pas ici, les pamplemousses.

M.D. si verts et doux les pamplemousses

E. Pas d'allure, cher singe.

M.D. je ne suis pas singe, je suis fille de MIM, je suis Malenka
Dotchka

E.   Then ... you're me! MIM, Marja, my mom! It's me, I'm her daughter! How she loved Perry Como ... and Dean Martin!

   She announces ...

   F. *and* **E.** *sing, softly.*

E.   Donc tu es moi ! MIM, Maria, ma mère ! c'est moi, je suis sa
      fille ! Elle aimait tant Perry Como . . . et Dean Martin !

          Elle annonce . . .

      Ave Maria, by Perry Como

          F. *et* **E.** *chantent, doucement.* **U.** *enters and joins.*

      Ave Maria
      Gratia plena
      Maria, gratia plena
      Maria, gratia plena
      Ave, ave dominus
      Dominus ta-boom
      Benedicta tu in merveilles
      Et benedictus
      Et benedictus fructus vendredi
      Ventris tuae, ventris whoa
      Ave Maria

      Ave Maria
      Nunc et in hora mortis
      Et in hora mortis nostrae ora pro nobis
      peccadoribus
      Ave Maria

          F. *goes silent, exits, returns with the cat vase and places*
          it solemnly by the field. **E.** *watches.* **U.** *watches E.*

ACT TWO, Scene 5 (Universe of Ptolemy)

          Lights up on **E.** *alone. Chairs still lie overturned*
          behind her.

E.   Sometimes I want to climb up and up. I want to climb past
      all the answers, and past my mother, who didn't go so far up,

                                        That
Alberta place where her parents spent the war in sorrows and
frail hopes. She fled that place, my mother did.

                                        I let memory
construct my body using very few tools: paper, shoes, worn
stuffed animals.

            Grandma!

even though she may be in ashes and in heaven, which is to say, not on earth. Who was this woman my mother? Why did she flee her birth and forebears, flee the farm on the mountain and embrace the terrain of *The Dean Martin Show*? Is this what it is to be an immigrant, a Canadian? Is this what it is to integrate in another country?

I don't want to integrate here. I was born here, and I can't integrate. There are too many unsolved questions.

My mother kept just one photograph of the farm and horse. She loved that horse! King! She cut her horse out of the photograph and threw away the farm where she had grown. She did this as an adult. Those worn slumped wood buildings saddened her, she didn't want them following her . . . In them, for her, there was no human song.

But I remember the farm behind the horse. And now I am the only one to remember the photo. The snow and the wooden buildings on the berry mountain. The place hard to live in. Ce lieu albertain où ses parents ont passé la guerre dans la tristesse et dans le frêle espoir. Ma mère s'est enfuie de ce lieu-là. Sometimes I want to climb up and up. Past all the treelines in the universe. Past the ashes. Past the niches. Past the words and the poems and the ideas and the histories. Far past those who love me. I want to climb up and up. I don't know where I am going. I am not going anywhere. Je laisse la mémoire construire mon corps à partir de très peu d'outils : papier, souliers, vieilles peluches.

> *She turns a chair upright and slumps into it and finds the cabbage leaf and puts it on her head again and addresses the cat vase beside the field.*

I don't know any of the old songs. No one taught me. I didn't know who she was. She didn't teach me her mother's language. MIM ! Grand-mère !

(sings) Everybody loves somebody, sometime. . . .

F. steps out and puts makeup on **E.** *and dresses her in a grey dress of her mother's, which just looks strange on her.* **E.** *takes out her phone and uses its reverse camera as a mirror to see how she looks.*

On the phone screen is a projection of the **Universe of Ptolemy**, *like the crosscut of a cabbage. Ptolemy means her mother. Because the earth stands still and all the stars and planets move around her mother's love.*

E. *goes back and lies down behind the stove on the bench like a peasant, setting down the mirror-phone.* **F.** *opens the firebox and puts another log in . . . pokes, then satisfied, goes to turn out the light.*

The projection of **Ptolemy's universe** *appears on the back wall. Lights gradually go dim but for the image and the light onstage from the fire in the stove. All is quiet and still for a few seconds, then the huge image begins to fade.*

... no one in our house
ever drank martinis, or showed up in tuxedos, except Johnny-
next-door, who repaired cars in a real garage and had no
children. His brother had children, all girls. All of them in
wheelchairs! You see why Dean Martin terrified me. In our
house we had only the horse King, cut out of a photo, to save
us! My brothers had broken the back of the sofa, tussling
endlessly in the living room. Then we'd watch television and,
on the screen, our ordinary living room touched Dean Martin's
living room.

My mother was seduced. She made us listen to Dean Martin.
She laughed at Joe Levitch, his sidekick, Jerry Lewis. At such
times, we knew that my mother was someone else, she wasn't
only our mother. She came from nowhere, and she had a

ACT TWO, Scene 6 (Dean Martin)

> *As the cabbage spiral vanishes,* **F1** *and* **F2** *enter a-clatter lugging a Dean Martin cowhide couch², place it comically, yes no yes, like this, no . . . like this, perfect. They see the overturned chairs, and push them to one side. They wink ridiculously.* **Fs** *sprawl on the sofa and grin and test it to the sound of canned applause. They agree it's good, then exit, re-enter with martinis, and sit. Lights up on mezzanine of stage, like the set of* The Dean Martin Show. *What a chutzpah scene! As if another play has invaded our cabaret.*

Fs. Last night I slept like a baby! *(imitating Dean Martin gestures, clutching their bow ties, pursing lips . . . touching their hair)* . . . I woke up this morning with a bottle in my mouth . . . Crawl and don't crawl!

> **F1** *and* **F2** *straighten imaginary bow ties and slap their knees, laughing.* **E.** *wakes up behind the stove, sees them, speaks.*

E. Fright of fright. My mother in her Dean Martin phase frightened me . . . she was not one of us . . . personne chez nous ne buvait de martinis, ou ne se présentait en smoking, sauf Johnny-d'à-côté, qui réparait des voitures dans un vrai garage et n'avait pas d'enfants. Son frère avait des enfants, que des filles. Toutes en fauteuils roulants ! Vous voyez la raison de ma terreur face à Dean Martin. Chez nous on n'avait que la photo du cheval King, sans fond de scène, pour nous protéger ! Mes frères ont même brisé le dossier du sofa, se chamaillant sans cesse dans le salon. Puis on regardait la télévision et, à l'écran, notre salon normal touchait le salon de Dean Martin.

Ma mère a été séduite. Elle nous a fait écouter Dean Martin. Elle riait à Joe Levitch, le comparse de Dean, Jerry Lewis. On savait à ces moments-là que ma mère était quelqu'un d'autre, elle n'était pas que notre mère. Elle venait de nulle part, et

boyfriend on TV, a boyfriend in an American tuxedo, a crooner who sang to her and to us, a guy with curly hair that shone from the comb who sipped a martini and sang to us . . .

> **MIM** *enters with an* **F.** *and puts an end to this invented nostalgia.* **E.** *stands up while MIM declaims.*

MIM.   SAP OF APPLES!

E.   I was born in the kerosene of your gaze, Mom!

MIM.   YOU HAVE NO RIGHT!

E.   . . . an excavation of the presence of a language that coincides with light, the body as reason and intention lost,

elle avait un *boyfriend* à la télé, un mec en smoking américain, un crooner qui chantait pour elle et pour nous, un gars aux cheveux brillants et bouclés qui buvait un martini en nous chantant . . .

> **MIM** *entre avec un* **F.** *et met fin à toute cette nostalgie inventée.* **E.** *se lève pendant que MIM déclame.*

MIM. ALL EXCEPT LESS!
LESS MORE!
MORE LESS!
ABSTINENCE CHRONICAL!
PISS IN BOOTS!
IN BOUTIQUES!
DENY THE RIGHT TO DIE!
PHYSICAL!
PTOLEMY!
TRIGONOMETRY!
DISPROVEN THEORIES OF THE STARS!

> **2 Fs** *rush on noisily to remove cowhide couch. The martini drinkers help. They return to move the bench from behind the stove to where the couch was. One F. sees* **E.**'*s phone and tosses it onto the bench. It falls.* **MIM** *curses at their interruption.*

MIM. JUS DE POMME !

> **E.** *moves centre toward* **MIM**.

E. Je suis née dans le kérosène de ton regard, Maman !

MIM. TU N'AS PAS LE DROIT ! *(exits)*

> **E.** *sits on the bench.*

E. . . . une excavation de la présence d'un langage qui coïncide avec la lumière, le corps comme raison et intention égarée,

I enter the room, the room is memory, anonymous before my entrance, a room creates its anonymity, there are the surfaces of bodies, of furniture, and my body sleeping, surface among surfaces ... sleep, sleep.

Sleep weighs on life, it's said, but no, I didn't come to sleep but to register the thin layers of skin, the skin dreams of being organ, wants to come off unscathed, intact, and with this skin I make gestures:

carbon, effaced,

serene, leaving
without wanting to trespass on my own memories nor on those of my mother, nor those of my grandmother
I'm simply skin and ash,
ash of a charred house ...

and I can't go outside to play with my brothers. I can only stay here behind my grandmother's stove just as the peasants lay down in their beds during the monstrous murderous Soviet famine to conserve their energies and thus resist genocide. I'm waiting ...

> **MIM** *enters with a sheet of paper and reads aloud, mockingly, in an almost falsetto voice (for it's a text by E.):*

MIM. Monkeys have always been oppressed by lions!
And the lioness roars: origin! origin!
See what I mean? oppressed by lionesses.
But this isn't a lioness, it's a plush toy ...

> *The monkey* **M.D.** *arrives between* **E.** *and the public in a stroller launched from offstage; E. tries to stop it and M.D. falls, back toward the public.*

j'entre dans la pièce, la pièce est la mémoire, anonyme avant mon entrée, une pièce fait son anonymat, il y a les surfaces des corps, des meubles, et mon corps endormi, une surface parmi d'autres ... sommeil, sommeil. To let dust and ash seep. I walk in sun's solace and look, link surety, passing through water in my membrane self.

Le sommeil pèse sur la vie, on dirait, mais non, je ne suis pas ici pour dormir mais pour sentir les couches minces de la peau, la peau qui se veut organe, se veut indemne, intacte, et avec cette peau je pose des gestes :

charbons, effacés,

sereine, laissant la « literature to itself »
sans vouloir m'introduire dans mes propres souvenirs ni dans ceux de ma mère, ni ceux de ma grand-mère
je ne suis que peau et cendre,
cendre d'une maison incendiée ...

et je ne peux aller jouer dehors avec mes frères. Je ne peux que rester ici derrière le poêle de ma grand-mère comme les paysans sont restés au lit pendant la grande famine meurtrière soviétique pour conserver leurs forces et ainsi résister au génocide. J'attends ...

> **MIM** *entre avec une feuille de papier et lit à haute voix, presque de fausset, se moquant du texte (car il s'agit d'un texte d'E.) :*

MIM. Les singes ont toujours été opprimés par les lions !
Et la lionne rugit : origine, origine !
Mais tu vois ? opprimés par les lionnes.
Mais là, ce n'est pas une lionne, c'est une peluche ...

> *Le singe **M.D.** arrive sur scène entre **E.** et le public dans une poussette projetée depuis les coulisses ; E. tente de l'arrêter et M.D. tombe, le dos vers le public.*

SCANDAL!
ALL BUT LESS!
LESS OF MORE!
MORE OF LESS!
CHRONIC ABSTINENCE!
PUSS IN BOOTS!! MAISTER CAT!

> *Meanwhile, from the field, another voice, the voice of* **Jan Eeyore**, *illuminated* . . .

MIM.   IN BOUTIQUES!
DENY THE RIGHT TO DIE!
PHYSICS!
PTOLEMY!
TRIGONOMETRY!
REFUTED THEORIES OF THE STARS!

E.   (*looks at her, quietly*)

MIM.   She's clearly an imbecile, see, the author of this play . . .

E.   um, Mom . . .

MIM.   I'm *MIM*.

E.   um, MIM . . . um, and Dean Martin, your boyfriend?

MIM.   He's not my boyfriend, dear. He never was . . .

song #2 *by* **M.D.**, *who cannot sing* ◁))

SCANDALE !
TOUT SAUF MOINS !
MOINS DE PLUS !
PLUS DE MOINS !
ABSTINENCE CHRONIQUE !
PISSE EN BOTTINES !! MAISTRE CHAT !

En même temps, du champ, une autre voix, celle de
Jan Eeyore, *illuminé . . .*

J.EE. « they trace their hands with pigment and breath »

« theirs was the cave where repetition's gesture was born »

« they lay down in their beds in August '33 »

MIM. EN BOUTIQUE !
NIER LE DROIT À MOURIR !
PHYSIQUE !
PTOLÉMÉE !
TRIGONOMÉTRIE !
THÉORIES RÉFUTÉES DES ÉTOILES !

E. (*la regarde, silencieuse*)

MIM. Qu'elle est débile, tu vois, l'auteure de cette pièce . . .

E. bon, Maman . . .

MIM. Je suis *MIM*.

E. bon, MIM . . . et Dean Martin, ton *boyfriend* ?

MIM. Il n'est pas mon mec, chérie. Il ne l'a jamais été . . .

Lights dim and remain just on **M.D.** *with her back toward the public.*

chant n° 2 *de* **M.D.**, *qui ne peut pas chanter* 🔊

INTERMISSION

2 for an image of a Dean Martin couch: 🖵 *www.youtube.com/watch?v=HyRlb1Fzv2M*

E. Does M.D. feel anguish? No, no, M.D. feels exactly nothing.
M.D. is a monkey doll made out of a grey winter sock. As such,
M.D., properly speaking, cannot speak.

POETRY IS A FEELING OF A STATE OF LANGUAGE
THAT GRATES IN THE THROAT. *(projected)*

U. It is a country of beautiful forests and drunken boys. The
Ukrainian poet (not drunk) read a beautiful poem, almost
chanted it in the metal ring or outcry of church bells, but
with something anti-Semitic in it. So. The American heard
it. Later I saw it, in reading. Did I get on the wrong train?
I worked on trains, I am terrified of them. Hundreds of
thousands were deported on trains. Millions, deported on
trains. France was deported on a train. Hungary, on a
train. Ukraine, no: only part of Ukraine left on a train.
Ukraine that was not! Ukraine that was forced to be Poland!
Today we sit in our sushi restaurants and we grieve! We sing
our ashes! We wear these strips of cloth we call our clothes.
Incense or metonymy! Shades solemnal! Abscess in the
mouth! Sewer grate! I am so terrified. When they crowded
people like that into the railcars, they had already lost
their names. Chalked numbers, calcified origins.

ACT THREE: POLLEN
Scene 1 (many aprons)

> **E.** *is at the stove. Muttering to herself. Cooking in the pot. The stage is clear, apart from stove, pot, and tarp laid on the floor to mark the field.* **M.D.** *is downstage on the floor.*

E. M.D. ressent-elle de l'angoisse ? Non, M.D. ne ressent précisément rien. M.D. est une poupée-singe faite d'une chaussette d'hiver grise. M.D., à proprement parler, ne parle pas.

> LA POÉSIE EST LA SENSATION D'UN ÉTAT DE LANGAGE QUI RACLE LA GORGE. *(projeté)*

> **U.** *enters and picks up* **M.D.** *The projected words dissolve as U. speaks.*

U. C'est un pays de belles forêts et de jeunes gars ivres. Le poète ukrainien (pas ivre) a récité un poème éblouissant, l'a quasi chanté dans le son métallique ou le cri des cloches, mais il y avait quelque chose d'antisémite dans le poème. Bon. L'Américain l'a entendu. Plus tard, je l'ai vu, en lisant. Est-ce que je suis montée à bord du mauvais train ? J'y ai travaillé, à bord des trains, les trains me terrifient. Des gens, des centaines de milliers ont été déportés dans des trains. Des millions, déportés dans des trains. La France a été déportée dans un train. La Hongrie, dans un train. L'Ukraine ? Seule une partie de l'Ukraine. L'Ukraine qui n'a jamais existé ! L'Ukraine forcée à être la Pologne. Aujourd'hui, on s'assoit dans nos restos de sushi et on fait son deuil ! On chante des cendres ! On porte ces bandes de tissu qu'on appelle nos vêtements. Encens ou métonymie ! Ombres solennelles ! Abcès dans la bouche ! Bouche d'égout ! Je suis si terrifiée. Quand on les a entassés dans les wagons, ces gens avaient déjà perdu leurs noms. Origines calcifiées, numéros à la craie.

They didn't even count them! They stuffed them into the cars and the Germans just guessed at their numbers. Even the chalk numbers on the wagon doors had nothing more to do with human beings. I beg of you.

Tomato

paste!

On ne les a même pas comptés. Les Allemands les ont fourrés dans des wagons et en ont estimé le nombre. Même les chiffres à la craie n'avaient plus rien à voir avec des êtres humains. Je vous en prie.

*U. exits, carrying **M.D.** tenderly. Silence. Then . . .*

E.   I fell into her whispers.

*Silence. **E.** shakes her head. Silence.*

I went deaf in the ears. Box sandwich! Ramen! Coulis de tomate ! I went grey in the temples, grey at the throat! Solitude of the stars! You think you are with someone but you are alone. Fundamentally, piss-dry basin of regret! Try again. Salute an onion! Make yourself rich in a jar! Fortitude! Lost heart! When we tried to be . . . when we . . . when . . . Tryptophan in the north! Hello Kitty knew me too. Cough, sputter, silence. Brigade of eaters!

Silence.

Old collapse! Modernity! The North! I ache! I hate you!

*Silence. **E.** shakes her head, holding and hitting her ear.*

I have a disease caused by chemicals and the voice. I ate diseased vegetables and cattle. I was no worse off. They tried to serve me orange juice, which made me sicker. Up one side and down another! Try again! The leaves were too big, they were gorged with water. I was attacked, I smoked, I did not dare return to the building so I had no jacket. I plunged into the woods. I boiled chestnuts and ate even the skin. I was sick on plants. I cried, I threw up, I danced with the others, following the strange movements of their limbs in the hills, mimicking so they would not betray me. I was unable to say how long I had been in the forest without water. I ate the

leaves. Skin came off my fingers. I fell in love with a girl and I was a girl. In the dark, I sobbed. In the day, I carpet-bombed life with my demons, no one could see me. I could switch, my bones hurt, the tumours had come back, I threw them up in the toilet, I was still on the train, I was never on a train. The train had no toilet.

We moved into the water. We moved into the air as ashes of our houses! The ones with the trident caps burned our skins off. The ones in the trident caps fought tyranny the only way they knew how! Burn even the trees! *(derisory)* Polish trees! *(serious)* I crouched in the field, I was eight years old, I was two, my sister strangled me to stop me from crying out and now she is alive and I am dead and there is no one to hear me. After the Jews had gone, onto the trains or into the forest, it was we who were sought out, because of a name, a sound of a name, because of an h in a nhame, because of a word for food!

> *Phones ring, seemingly in the public.* **E.** *steps toward the edge of the stage, startled, recognizing her.*

Malenka Dotchka. Speak!

> *An* **iPhone** *lowers on a cable centre stage. It plays* Маленька Дочка's **Song #1** *in a very tinny voice.*
>
> **F.** *comes out to centre stage with a bucket and* **E.** *turns and throws up in it.* **F2** *comes out with a glass and a bucket of water, and helps E. try to get water into the glass; finally they pull the dead leaves out of the bucket and then pour water into the glass and E. drinks it and phones are ringing, cacophony. F2 runs offstage.* **M.D.**'s *voice has gone silent.*
>
> **E.** *speaks into the dangling phone and the voice projects:*

Our houses filled up with water. We were in the water. We could not swim. They lowered our furniture to the street on cables. We could not swim. We could not scream or they would kill us too.

Lies!

MIM. STINKWORD!

E. Courage, Mom! You weren't even there! You were in Alberta. No one burned the village, it was just a few houses. You weren't even there. Nor was your father, nor your mother. Here, in Alberta, your parents bore their burden of sorrow but all of you were unscathed!

MIM. STINKWORD! Shut up!

POETRY IS THE SENSATION OF A STATE OF
LANGUAGE CRAWLING OUT OF THE EAR. *(projected)*

I'm lying. Mensonge !

> *F2 returns with* **MIM**, *both sitting on the Dean Martin couch pushed by* **2 other Fs**. **E.** *turns to watch MIM. The phone sways on its cord like a pendulum.*

MIM. MALVERBE !

E. Courage, Maman ! Tu n'étais pas là ! T'étais en Alberta. Personne n'a brûlé le village, ils ont brûlé à peine quelques maisons. Tu n'étais même pas là. Ni ton père ni ta mère. Ici en Alberta, tes parents ont eu un grand chagrin mais vous étiez tous indemnes !

MIM. MALVERBE ! Tais-toi !

> **E.** *shuts up . . . a sleepy hoarse voice of* **MIM** *is heard from the dangling phone. It speaks then goes silent.*

iPhone. Many *APRONS!* There has to be *many aprons!*
And she adds: But I'm little!
Then the figurant comes on with aprons and E. cries out: You're not *little!*
I want to be *little!*
You're *not* little!
Then she goes behind the stove and lies down to make herself little.

> **F1** *enters and leaves with both buckets.* **F2** *exits with* **MIM**, *pushing the couch. The phone rises. F2 returns with MIM walking; MIM holds* **Маленька Дочка**.

MIM. You were always bigger than me. Even when you were littler than me, you were bigger.

(*looks up*) Something is trying to crawl out of my ear!

> LA POÉSIE EST LA SENSATION D'UN ÉTAT DE LANGAGE FOURMILLANT DE L'OREILLE. (*projeté*)

F1 returns with a huge pile of aprons and then takes **M.D.** *from MIM.* **E.** *and MIM gaze together at the aprons.*

E.   You are not little, Mom.

MIM.   But I WANT to be little.

E.   You're not little!

> **E.** *leaves* **MIM** *and lies behind the stove to make herself little. MIM and* **F1** *are alone downstage. MIM continues to shake her head.*

E.   *(quietly)* We're all little. How else to live?

Fabrication!
Lies!

"All spiritual joy can be expressed by eating food." Novalis, *Fragmentos*, tr. from German by sculptor Rui Chafes)

> **E.** *walks distractedly and slowly over the field-tarp;*

E.   I see with his eyes (Félix)
     so I am his child
     I can recite Kaddish for him
     in fact, I must

     and that's how I started
     to believe in the world again
     and the name
     gaze
     eyes

> **MIM** *shakes her head as if trying to get water out of her ear.* **F1** *revient avec une montagne de tabliers et prend* **M.D.** *de MIM.* **E.** *et MIM regardent les tabliers.*

E.   Tu n'es pas petite, Maman.

MIM.   Mais je VEUX être petite.

E.   Tu n'es pas petite !

> **E.** *quitte* **MIM** *et se couche derrière le poêle pour se faire petite. MIM et* **F1** *restent seuls en avant-scène. MIM continue de secouer la tête.*

E.   *(doucement)* On est tous petits. Comment vivre, d'ailleurs ?

Fabrication !
Mensonge !

> *Lights dim on* **E.** *then go down on* **MIM** *and* **F1***.*

ACT THREE, Scene 2 « Todo o gozo espiritual se pode exprimir pelo comer. » Novalis, *Fragmentos*, tr. do alemão por Rui Chafes)

> **E.** *marche distraitement et lentement sur le bâche-champ ; on the far side of the stage, the pot steams on the stove. The pile of aprons is now on the tarp.* **M.D.** *is back in her spot on the floor downstage. E. sings then speaks.*

E.   Je vois avec ses yeux (Félix)
     donc je suis son enfant
     je peux réciter le Kaddisch pour lui
     en fait, je dois le faire

     et c'est comme ça que j'ai
     recommencé à croire au monde
     et au nom
     le regard
     les yeux

in the Old Country.

```
On arrival at the camp,
the grandmothers took the little ones in their arms
so their mothers could live.
```

"Anyone in my place would confirm my
testimony."

But where do you come from, Mom? We're Polish. We're
Ukrainian. We're nothing. From nowhere!

"The singular instant, insofar as it can be repeated, becomes
an ideal instant."

Too many opinions!
Pride of nature!
Overwrought nativity!

F1.   And in Lvov-Lviv, apart from the trains, 200,000 shot,
      46 thousand in 3 days, 49 pits. It's human history! It's
      Ukrainian history. Their bones still scream and stir the
      earth! Our bones. Our lips. Our mouths, our tongues! Earthly
      screams!

      We forget, we go on, there are mitigating factors; there are
      reasons, historical and other, for these behaviours — there
      are excuses. Me, I tolerate all these excuses. But the bones of
      innocent people still squirm and churn the earth.

E.   They're bones. Microbes! Particles of DNA! They're in solidarity,
      those bones, with the air, with the climate! with the leaves

In the Bear Creek Valley at Grande Prairie, bears. Nearby in
Beaverlodge, fine grass and deer. First leaves of spring on
our aspens. But the first leaves I saw this year were not there
but at Birkenau-Auschwitz. In Cracovie, at the castle. In Lvov-
Lviv, au Vieux Pays. That yellow tinge just before the leaves
break open.

En arrivant au camp,
les grand-mères ont pris les petits dans leurs bras
afin que leurs mères puissent vivre.

« N'importe qui à ma place confirmerait mon
témoignage. »

Mais d'où viens-tu, Maman ? On est Polonais. On est
Ukrainiens. On n'est rien. De nulle part !

« L'instant singulier, dans la mesure où il est répétable,
devient un instant idéal. »

Toutes ces opinions !
Orgueil de la nature !
Nativité surfaite !

> **F1** *returns and approaches* **E.** *as if to calm her. But then
> loses calm as words crawl out of her ear . . .*

F1. Et à Lvov-Lviv, outre les trains, 200 000 fusillés, 46 000 en
trois jours ; 49 fosses. C'est une histoire humaine ! C'est une
histoire ukrainienne. Leurs os crient toujours et remuent la
terre ! Nos os. Nos lèvres. Nos bouches, nos langues ! Des cris
terrestres !

On oublie, on continue, il y a des facteurs atténuants ; il y a des
raisons, historiques et autres, pour de tels comportements —
il y a des excuses. J'admets, moi, toutes les excuses. Mais les
os des innocents continuent à remuer la terre.

E. Ils sont des os. Des microbes ! Des particules d'ADN ! Ils sont
solidaires, ces os-là, avec l'air, avec le climat ! avec les feuilles

that emerge! With my mouth and with my lips. My throat, my ears!

> MIM *enters, in her nurse's uniform, with* **F2**. *She approaches* **E.** *and stops, examines her for a moment before speaking.*

MIM.   Don't wear your shoes in the house. Take them off!

E.   *(steps out of the field and takes her shoes off)*

MIM.   No shoes inside the house! Show some respect for the work of your mother.

MIM.   No. *(quiet)*

Malenka Dotchka was never littler than me!

MIM.   I'll leave you money under the salt shaker, dear, so you can buy food for yourself and your brothers. We always had lots of food to eat. *(proud and insistent)* No one ever went hungry in this house.

qui émergent ! Avec ma bouche et avec mes lèvres. Ma gorge,
mes oreilles !

> **MIM** *entre en tenue d'infirmière avec* **F2**. *Elle s'approche
> de* **E**. *et s'arrête, la regarde un moment avant de parler.*

MIM. Ne porte pas tes souliers dans la maison. Enlève-les !

E. *(sort du champ et enlève ses souliers)* Maty, do you remember
running uphill in the village between the houses where you
were born?

MIM. Pas de souliers dans la maison ! Il faut respecter le travail de
ta mère.

E. Do you remember running uphill in the village of Great
Breadville? You were four . . .

MIM. Non. *(silencieuse)*

E. But I remember when *I* was four. I already knew how to read!
I remember you, my mother! You stood at the sink in the
kitchen and helped me read!

MIM. You taught yourself how to read. Malenka Dotchka n'a jamais
été plus petite que moi !

E. I was in Ukraine to see my grandmother's land, Mom. In
front of the Opera in the great city Lvov-Lviv I stood and
wondered. Patterns of water. Trees! I went to the village.
Leaves and throats. 1,200 were marched through your village,
Mom, to enter the trains. Do you know why grandmother was
sad? The neighbours told her in the letters! Leaves and ears!
Your parents read the letters aloud to each other in whispers
at night and you heard. We can't live as broken beings, Mom.
We have to do better!

MIM. Je te laisserai de l'argent sous la salière, chérie, afin que tu
puisses acheter de quoi manger pour toi et pour tes frères. On
a toujours eu de quoi manger. *(fière et insistante)* On n'a jamais
eu faim dans cette maison.

E.   (*screams*) shoeless salt shaker shameless shits!

(White-tailed Deer and Shoes)

E. *standing beside the field,*

E.   I saw deer in the fields of cabbages and grains. In their mouths they took the seeds and leaves of plants that grew out of the soil. It's winter and snow covers the grains. The ashes from sewing machines cover the grain like pepper. Coloured flecks.

I lost barley here somewhere, in '43, in '42. In '42 in the RKU, innocents later called Soviet citizens had already been killed. The Jews. And after the Jews, it was the so-called Poles. Those men and women who had an accent, a way of pronouncing the word for God, for cabbage. Another calendar. Even in the mixed villages. We no longer existed. Kapusta! Neither us nor the barley. We don't even know anymore who we are. We ring inside like telephones, and no one answers!

No more letters arrived in Alberta after the war.

```
Cover me, pale stalks of barley.
Cover me, my ashes worn,
my own ashes warm.
Forget me
Nothing. Forget nothing, storm.
```

E. (*crie*) sans souliers salière salauds !

MIM *exits with* **F2**.

ACT THREE, Scene 3 (Chevreuils et souliers)

> **E.** *debout à côté du champ, her back to the stove and main part of the stage. She wears the hat. The pot is stirred by an* **F.** *now, who tastes what is in it. The table is back, set for dinner. Lit. The bench is at the table. Other* **Fs** *are at the table.* **M.D.** *is downstage on the floor.*

E. J'ai vu des chevreuils dans les champs de choux et de blés. Dans leurs bouches ils ont pris les graines et les feuilles des plantes qui poussaient du sol. C'était l'hiver et la neige couvrait les blés. Les cendres des machines à coudre couvraient la neige comme du poivre. Coloré.

J'ai perdu de l'orge ici quelque part, en '43, en '42. En '42 dans le RKU, les innocents étaient déjà morts, les « citoyens de l'État soviétique » comme ils ont dit plus tard. Les Juifs ! Et après les Juifs en '42, c'était les présumés Polonais. Ceux et celles qui avaient un accent, une manière de prononcer le mot pour Dieu, pour choux. Un autre calendrier. Même dans les villages mixtes. Nous n'existions plus. Kapusta ! Ni nous ni l'orge. On ne sait même plus qui on est. On sonne de l'intérieur comme des téléphones, sans réponse !

Les lettres n'arrivaient plus en Alberta après la guerre.

> *Then to the tune of a fake Dean Martin song:*

```
Couvre-moi, orge.
Couvre-moi, avec mes cendres,
mes propres cendres.
Oubliez-moi
Rien. N'oubliez rien, orage.
```

(speaks) When I hear this song I learned as a child,
I am some kind of crazy choir.

MIM.　*(to M.D.)* Do you remember your pyjamas?

> *The **Fs**, on seeing the pyjamas, scream,*

Fs.　Avoid the sick!
Get away from the sick!

> *An **F**. starts to sneeze and sniffle; the others move their
> chairs away a little. **E**. arrives at the edge of the field,
> staring at the heap of aprons. She speaks slowly, in a soft
> voice, her eyes glued to the field.*

E.　They took the rotting corpses from the pits to kill them
another time, to make them disappear. By fire. It's
true. You could catch a disease from those corpses! They
planted the forests later, at Lisinitchi, Lvov-Lviv, to hide
everything.

The bonfires were day and night
a layer of bodies
a layer of wood

a layer of bodies
200 bodies on each bonfire

46,000 in 3 days, 49 pits, for months, corpses without
human song

(parle) Quand j'entends ce chant que j'ai appris enfant,
je suis un choeur détraqué.

> An **F.** *exits and comes back with* **MIM**, *who bears
> pyjamas for* **Маленька Дочка**.

MIM. *(à M.D.)* Te souviens-tu de ton pyjama ?

M.D. *(M.D. does not speak, properly speaking)*

> Les **Fs**, *en voyant le pyjama, crient, offstage and/or
> at the table :*

Fs. Évitez les malades !
Écartez-vous des malades !

> *Un* **F.** *commence à éternuer et à renifler : les autres
> éloignent leurs chaises un peu. Arrivée au bord du champ,*
> **E.** *regarde le tas de tabliers. Elle parle lentement, à voix
> basse, ses yeux fixés sur le champ.*

E. Ils ont pris les corps pourris des fosses pour les tuer encore
une fois, pour les faire disparaître. Par le feu. C'est vrai. On
peut attraper des maladies avec ces cadavres ! Les forêts à
Lisinitchi, Lvov-Lviv, ils les ont plantées après, pour tout
cacher.

Les brasiers étaient jour et nuit
une couche de corps
une couche de bois

une couche de corps
200 corps sur chaque brasier

46 000 en 3 jours, 49 fosses, pendant des mois, des cadavres
sans chant humain

> *Silence.*

U. enters and turns to **Маленька Дочка** *who is utterly still, and pulls her away from* **MIM** *to centre, back facing the public, then pulls out a book or paper, salutes* **M.D.**, *and declaims to the public (* **E.** *watches, one* **F.** *keeps stirring the pot) . . .*

U.   Words stolen from Heiner Müller as Маленька Дочка, strictly speaking, does not speak!

M.D.   (*read by* **F2** *who approaches, shadowed*)

— What would you regard as a central issue in your recent texts?
— How should I know, and if I knew why should I tell you?
— If you reject this idea of a central issue, could you mention some of the interests you pursue in your writing?
— See above.

U.   Words stolen from Emmanuel Lévinas as Маленька Дочка, strictly speaking, does not speak!

M.D.   — The face is not "seen." It is what cannot become a content, which your thought would embrace; the face is uncontainable, it leads you beyond.

U.   Words stolen from Nadezhda Mandelstam as Маленька Дочка, strictly speaking, does not speak!

M.D.   — Peasants just lay quite still in their houses. We all do this. I have spent my whole life lying down.

Silence. They switch roles suddenly.

M.D.   Words stolen from Judith Butler as Маленька Дочка, strictly speaking, does not speak!

U.   — The back is a scene of agonized vocalization.

M.D.   Words stolen from Istvana Poltmanova as Маленька Дочка, strictly speaking, does not speak!

U.   — Poetry is a feeling of a state of language seared in the throat.

U. — A testimony can be false, that is, in error, without being false testimony, that is, without involving perjury, lies, the deliberate attempt to deceive.

E. *impatient, interrupts* . . .

E. Stop, stop! This is no place to sing! It's not a synagogue! nor a church nor a stadium! it's a cemetery! Here the bones of innocent people still shake the earth and demand justice!

We have our regrets! We tower over everything from our huge heights, and there is still passivity in the face of genocides! do your best! respect your mother! chew your food! take off your shoes when you come into this house!

(hurdy-gurdy)

U. Thunder! Episteme! Hedge! Varnish!

M.D. Words stolen from Jacques Derrida as Маленька Дочка, strictly speaking, does not speak!

U. — Un témoignage peut être faux, c'est-à-dire erroné, sans être un faux témoignage, c'est-à-dire sans impliquer le parjure, le mensonge, l'intention délibérée de tromper.

E. impatiente, l'interrompt . . .

E. Arrête, arrête ! Ça ne chante pas ici ! ce n'est pas une synagogue ni une église ni un stade ! c'est un cimetière ! Ici les os des innocents secouent encore la terre et demandent justice !

On a nos regrets ! On est si hauts qu'on domine tout, et il y a encore de la passivité face aux génocides ! fais de ton mieux ! respecte ta maman ! chew your food! enlève tes souliers dans cette maison !

ACT THREE, Scene 4 (boîte à musique)

Fs and U. in a row downstage on chairs in front of the large table. They are all in stocking feet. One F. is seated with the tiny piano; one holds an iPhone with the Virtuoso app open, and plays a discordant chord, entirely invented, and the Fs start speaking. Several at once, one at a time. Occasionally they fall silent for no reason. The pianist whacks a chord again and they start up. As if they were all part of a crazy music box or choir or cabaret.

E. is behind the stove, lying down on the bench.

U. enters as if to announce what is next. F. hits another chord.

U. Tonnerre ! Epistème ! Buisson ! Vernis !

Fs. Saints later failed them. Electric furuncle! My horse King! Obstinacy did prevail! 200 shot in the square for refusing to

Here, suffering! Here!

Living space!

Grease of Yalta!

walk to the railway station on August 12, 1942. 1,200–1,500 did walk, arriving in the village of Malenka Dotchka's mother, Great Breadville, can you imagine 1,200–1,500 souls arriving in a village? Clamour of silence! Clamour of no rest! On that day alone, the shut trains stopped in the village, on that day alone! Mercilessness mercy! Ici la souffrance, ici ! In Bełżec, no one cut their hair! In Bełżec, 15 minutes and poof! *Lebensraum!* I dare not look back lest I lose you forever!

The testimonies are given. The man talked of the cherries. The smallest of the children crawled out of the ghetto at night between the boards, Bibrka, Ukraine. A year of famine in 1942.

Niemçi. A big Star of David on every board. This poetry is not mood poetry! They found the pits of cherries fallen in the road and broke them with stones, to eat the pits. Later they died. What a spring! Peace of Riga! Later they were murdered! Even babes in arms. The seeds of the cherries were buried in them. That is why we did not grow up! That is why my mother is so small! There was no blood! They had to eat the grass like cattle. Then they were shot!

> One **F.** *rises and goes to pull the huge tarp-field closer,*
> *the aprons on it . . . pulls it in front of the row of chairs,*
> *between chairs and* **M.D.** *whose back still faces the public,*
> *heading to the stove at the far back of the stage.*
>
> *Seeing the tarpaulin,* **M.D.** *starts screaming (the light is*
> *on her and there is noise everywhere of this scream . . . in*
> *reality, she is just still).*

Some things shall arise from the depth of time! They also removed snow on the road to Lviv! Imagine! Graisse de Yalta ! Clearing a highway with snow shovels! The people of the village whose blood could not be killed by shooting, killed with these shovels! Inured to horror, the soil soaked with blood — to create a country? Ukraine! The war is over and it's no better! Yesterday the West, today the East!

Nuclear medicine!

Stomata! Soup tartare!

In 1942,
big famine here, the people of the village were starving.

Abscess of slime! Fanatics! Casualties! Médecine nucléaire !
Stomata ! Soupe de tartare ! Thank you Stalin!

> *Other **Fs** run offstage and return with the house set on fire*
> *with a phone for light inside it. The Fs hide their eyes. **E.***
> *emerges from behind the stove, puts the cabbage leaf and*
> *hat on, listens, shakes her head as if something is trying*
> *to come out of HER ear, and says quietly:*

E.   In the village, they'd put pillows in their windows at night to
muffle the cries of those being killed by those in German
uniform, no our police did not participate, yes the police did,
no it was only the Germans. No it was not, for it was we
brought their furniture down on cords! All dead and gone!
There was a snow. We were all hungry that year. En 1942,
grande famine ici, les gens du village crevaient de faim.
Requisitions of food when there was already none! A year
later, we too, you too, killed by the ones who want purity, who
want to stay alive, who want alone to live onward, those ones
with the ideal of Nation, the ones who survived every genocide,
determined, whose eyes sink forward not back into their
skulls, whose wounds wear wet salve, whose wounds wear
peppercorns and ashes, they are our killers too, some of them,
some of you. There's pain too when we see those trident caps!

> ***F.** holding the tarp stops pulling and looks at it in horror.*
> *Then rushes to fold it up and drag it to stuff it into the lit*
> *stove. It's too big, it's impossible. F. flounders. **MIM** enters*
> *with **F2**.*

MIM.   DISPROVEN THEORIES OF THE STARS!

> ***F.** stops and lets the tarp drop.*

MIM.   Some things still arise from the depth of time! In no way
imaginary! The blood came out of the fields, it smelled bad,
it ran down the hill into the road! Sob me with grass!

*F2 walks **MIM** to the edge of the stage, where she speaks in a softer voice, to the public, challenging them.*

There you are. Verbatim!

Why has it taken you so long to come?

Fs.   *(whisper aside)* Chalk in the fields. Alone, wept. So many bones already in the ground! Science of cows! Then they came at night and all men of honour donned those trident caps! My ancestors who freed me wore those caps! To be half-Polish was to be half-dead! And what was Polish? Neighbours? Those only half-Polish were cut in half, so as to kill only the Polish part: who then was wounded? The rest of the body is saved! Justice for birds! Luckily Oleks was already gone. Soup fester! Grandfather! Grandmother! Luckily you had long emigrated!

MIM *reaches* **Маленька Дочка** *again.*

MIM.   I'll leave you money under the salt shaker. In Calgary, our city. All you have to do is take it when you come back from school, and go to the store to buy bread for yourself and your brothers!

E. *steps close and stands near **MIM** and **M.D.** The **F.** with tarp retraces steps, helped by other **Fs** and lays the tarp where it originally was. It's useless to try to burn it.*

E.   Did anyone know where they went to? The ones who were left alive? The ones who lived, lived because they were silent? The ones who were baptized again? The ones who learned to say Maty forever, in Ukrainian? Who were we, Mother! MIM! Maty! Dissolve me now! Before I can hate!

MIM.   My parents cried at night. And would not tell us why. No one wrote ever again after the war. There were no letters after the war.

Deafening victory for the air!

Miroslav! Verbatim!

Suffering is here! Here! Right now I see white-tailed deer in the field here, here, eating the seeds of grain!

The **UNIVERSE OF PTOLEMY**

E. I went there to Olesko this year, Mom, I know that story! I saw the first leaves. I saw bones too, coming out of the snow! Women and children! Because they were Jews! League of Nations!

Then Yalta, thank you Churchill: the last brutality in a line of brutalities. Poles to Poland, Ukrainians to Ukraine. Purity of life! But the bodies of those before them still stank in the field. Their bones climb into the trees when the snow melts in spring! And when that war ended, Stalin sent even Ukrainians to Siberia. Unreliable border dwellers. Far east. No one triumphed. Shhhhhhh. Passivity of ash! Who are you? Who is left?

> **E.** *steps back and starts to dismantle the stove.* **Fs** *rise and encircle the tarp. E. continues, more softly.*

Ici la souffrance ! Ici ! Je vois en ce moment des chevreuils dans le champ ici, ici, en train de manger des céréales !

> **L'UNIVERS DE PTOLÉMÉE** *appears behind the players. All hold up lit phones.*

Where they got off the trains at Birkenau, during the war, there were sheds for potatoes! Potatoes! Apples of the ground that were stored and forced to nourish death. I hate you, potatoes! You said nothing, you lay there eyes shut without resisting that death.

ACT THREE, Scene 5 (the face)

> **E.** *is alone downstage. The stove is dismantled. The tarp
> still spread out. E. holds* **Leonne Orph,eu**, *the lioness.*

E.   I dare not look back lest I lose you forever. Orph,eu, lioness.
I too was bitten and bitten, my sword was bitten, my mouth
turned to sour jelly.

Their faces vanished at death. I dare not look back.

The saints later . . . failed them.

I am speaking through the intermediary of the face, of
my face.

I cannot face them.

> *Sings.*

```
The first time we sang a song
it was scar tissue
The second time we sang
it was joy
Shall I sing it another time?
Shall we sing the song again tomorrow?

Be mine, be mine sang the radio box speaker
sanguine

I forget the song, I don't know the song
Boots on, we're going (another memory like this)*
Door's wide, we're gone
```

Là où ils sont descendus des trains à Birkenau, durant la
guerre, il y avait des baraques pour emmagasiner les pommes
de terre ! Des pommes de la terre obligées d'alimenter la
mort. Je ne vous aime pas, patates ! Vous n'avez rien dit, vous
êtes restées là, les yeux fermés, sans résister à la mort.

*All the **Fs**, gathered around the tarp, put on masks*
*that bear **M.D.**'s face and start to speak, quietly,*
in the shadows . . .

Fs. We churn, we return, we repeat ourselves. How to refuse to
work for death? How could anyone work? Who could sow
wheat in such a field? At Bełżec, 37 Germans killed 501,000
human beings. Three survivors. With whose help? The people
around helped them. Prisoners of war were trained to be
guards . . . to eat, to save their families! 500 of them, of the
deportees, worked there too! The choice was no choice! Live
or die!

And after, the human pyres. The dead were killed twice. At
Lviv, little Orph,eu, our lioness, saw the loaded trucks drive
past! The Germans were losing the war; the survival of the
dead in the fields worried them. I can't stand it anymore.
Day and night near Lvov-Lviv at Lisinitchi they unloaded and
burned the bodies, for 3 months. The corpses were already
half-rotting. It stank everywhere! We saw the flames from
here. The flames were so high! We wrote all that down in the
letters we sent you! But you didn't do anything! There was
nothing left of human song!

They even requisitioned the villagers who owned horses to
transport bodies from the pits to the pyres.

We go in circles.
The women who were raped then shot, in a
forest. In a thicket.

*Tous les **Fs**, autour de la bâche, mettent des masques*
*qui portent le visage de **M.D.** et prennent la parole,*
calmement, dans l'ombre . . .

Fs. On se détourne, on retourne, on tourne en rond. Comment
refuser de travailler à la mort ? Comment travailler ?
Comment semer les blés dans un tel champ ? À Bełżec,
37 Allemands ont tué 501 000 personnes. Trois survivants. Avec
l'aide de qui ? Les gens autour les ont aidés. Des prisonniers de
guerre ont été formés pour être gardiens . . . pour manger,
pour épargner leurs familles ! 500 d'entre eux, les déportés,
ont travaillé aussi ! Le choix n'était pas un choix ! Vivre ou
mourir ! What sane person could understand it. . . .

Et après tous ces morts, les feux humains. On les a tués deux
fois. À Lviv, Orph, eu enfant, notre lionne, a vu le passage des
camions chargés ! Les Allemands étaient en train de perdre la
guerre ; la survie des morts dans les champs les préoccupait.
Je n'en peux plus. Jour et nuit près de Lvov-Lviv à Lisinitchi
ils ont déchargé et brûlé les corps, et ce pendant trois mois.
Les corps étaient déjà à moitié pourris. Ça puait ! On voyait le
feu d'ici. Les flammes étaient si hautes ! On a tout écrit dans
les lettres que nous vous avons envoyées ! Vous n'avez rien
fait ! Il n'y avait plus de chant humain !

Ils ont même réquisitionné les gens du village qui avaient des
chevaux pour amener les corps des fosses jusqu'aux bûchers.

The ones who had already left, alive? But they say they were
incinerated. They say: they went to Belz. On tourne en rond.
There was a snow. Le viol des filles, fusillées après, dans une
forêt. Dans un bosquet. They had to eat grass like cattle, and
drink from the river, then they were shot. 10 young villagers
dug the pit. The girls had to undress by the road then walk in
6 at a time, lie down, and be killed.

They started to cry out! They had to expel something! Shit or
bones! Killed with shovels! Their blood ran onto the roads at
night and in the day!

The villagers were forced to keep up their morale. We know it now. It's all known! We knew everything out in the berry bush, on the mountain! And no, no, no, there was nothing left of human song.

"It's fine, we're feeling fine" (or they would be killed).

Who? The boy called Baby who no longer knew his name; and the body counter, and the man who worked the grinder of the bones!

Later everything was covered up: they planted trees afterward.

We say no to monuments! "It's monuments that let us forget the dead."

MIM. We've come in the name of resistance to genocide. And we'll be back, we will return. The ultimate victory of the murderers and tyrants would be that no one returns.

Unclean!

MIM. Who's that with you? You're too big to be playing with dolls. Get rid of that crappy thing!

E. It's not crap, Mom. It's Leonne. It's Orph,eu the girl alive. She wants to thrive. She never wears shoes in the house and her house is the whole world.

We'd told some Ebreu to flee . . . you're going to your death, and they fled.

MIM. *(picked up by an **F**.)* Les villageois ont été condamnés à garder le moral. On le sait maintenant. Tout est connu ! On savait tout depuis les arbustes à petits fruits, sur la montagne ! Mais non, il n'y avait plus de chant humain.

« Tout va bien, tout va bien » (sinon, on les tuerait).

Qui? Le gars Baby qui ne connaissait plus son nom; et le compteur des corps, et l'homme qui a fait fonctionner le moulin à os !

Puis ils ont tout couvert: ils ont planté des arbres après.

On dit non aux monuments ! « C'est avec des monuments qu'on fait oublier les morts. »

MIM. On vient au nom de la résistance aux génocides. Et on revient, on reviendra. L'ultime victoire des assassins et des tyrans serait que personne ne revienne.

> *The **Fs** remove their M.D. sock-monkey masks and surround **E**. with their real faces. She holds the lioness's paw out to them and touches their cheeks.*

E. I don't know who has stolen my voice now, who wants to speak! Shit or bread! Shit or bones! Malpropre ! Triumph! Mom, is this somewhere? We can't come from nowhere!

> *She turns to face **MIM**.*

MIM. C'est qui ça avec toi ? Tu es trop grande pour jouer à la poupée. Laisse tomber cette patente ridicule !

E. Ce n'est pas une patente, Maty, c'est Lionne. C'est Orph,eu la fille en vie. Elle a envie de vivre. Elle ne porte jamais de souliers dans la maison et sa maison, c'est le monde.

> *Fs leave with **MIM**. Lights up on the salt shaker and **M.D.** **E**. sets down **Leonne Orph,eu** beside M.D.*

(filament of truth)

F. returns onstage with **MIM**, *and they approach* **E.** *The other* **Fs** *and* **U.** *enter behind them, quietly, shadowy, and lie down under the tarp while E. speaks to MIM.*

E.   *(admiringly)* You taught me how to read, Mom.

MIM.   We never went hungry in this house, Malenka Dotchka, never.

E.   You always left me money under the salt shaker, Mom. We always had good food. And we looked up at the stars in the firmament to name the constellations and you taught us how to tell time from the position of the sun.

MIM.   Go play outside with your brothers!

E.   My brothers are from here, Mom. They were never forced to be soldiers. My brothers are too young!

MIM.   We all stand responsible in the face of the other, Malenka Dotchka. We're all leaves of a single cabbage. Don't ever wear your shoes inside our house!

E.   You brought us up to be strong, Mom. And to take our shoes off in the house. I embrace you, Mom. I hug you with all my strength, for *I* received this strength from you so as to be able

ACT THREE, Scene 6 (fibre de vérité)

> **E.** *stands alone near the tarp which is spread out, still. She wears her mother's dress and the hat with the veil. The stove still dismantled. E. looks offstage after the departed* **MIM**. **M.D.**, *by the salt shaker, faces the public.* **L.O.** *is near her, and the action doll brothers. M.D.'s* **song #1**. *Then silence.*

> **F.** *appears onstage right in the near dark with a cart of cabbages, parks it at the edge of the stage, and leaves.*

E. (*excited voice, looking into the dark*) Maty! MIM!

> **E.** *realizes she is mistaken. Then . . .*

> **F.** *revient avec* **MIM**, *et s'approche de* **E.** *Les autres* **Fs** *et* **U.** *entrent derrière eux, silencieusement, ombrés, et se cachent sous la bâche pendant que E. parle à MIM.*

E. (*admiration*) Tu m'as appris à lire, Maman.

MIM. On n'a jamais souffert de faim dans cette maison, Malenka Dotchka, jamais.

E. Tu m'as toujours laissé de l'argent sous la salière, Maman. On a toujours bien mangé. Et on a regardé là-haut les étoiles pour nommer les constellations et tu nous as appris à déterminer l'heure à partir de la position du soleil.

MIM. Va jouer dehors avec tes frères !

E. Mes frères sont d'ici, Maman. Ils n'ont jamais été forcés d'être soldats. Mes frères sont trop jeunes !

MIM. On est tous responsables devant l'autre, Malenka Dotchka. On est des feuilles d'un seul et même chou. Ne porte jamais tes souliers dans notre maison !

E. Tu nous as appris à être forts, Maty. Et sans souliers dans la maison. Je t'embrasse, Maman. Je t'embrasse avec toutes mes forces, car *j'ai* reçu ces forces de toi afin d'être capable de

to decide, in the face of evil, to defend the plenitude of life, even if resistance could lead to death.

But the moment we face that death, that very moment, is not the moment when we give up our lives. We gave them up a long time ago, way back when we chose, come what may, to never turn our backs on plenitude and life.

Contradiction No!

Filament of truth Yes!

Barley!

Barely!

The corpses under the tarp stir a bit. **M.D.** *falls sideways.*

E.   (*screams at the corpses under the tarp*)

YOU'RE ALL DEAD!

U.   Even on Everest, the place on earth nearest to heaven, climbers who ascend to the highest point on our planet and this, almost without oxygen, walk past others who are dying from the pressure of their brains against their skulls, and they don't stop to help!

What makes you think the theatre is authentic?

Turn off your cellphones!

E.   You are my VOICE! Stop playing dead! Don't turn off anything! All ash ... all ash in us is *pollen*!

décider, face au mal, de défendre à haute voix la plénitude de la vie, même si cela pourrait entraîner la mort.

Mais le moment où on fait face à cette mort n'est pas le moment où on donne nos vies. On les a déjà données, il y a longtemps, quand on a choisi, quoi qu'il arrive, de ne jamais tourner le dos à la plénitude et à la vie.

Contradiction Non !

Fibre de vérité Oui !

MIM. (*shakes her head as if something is trying to crawl out of her ear*) De l'orge ! De l'orage !

> *The stage lights up brighter, sudden, blue. A flash. Les morts sous la bâche bougent un peu.* **M.D.** *tombe sur le côté.*

E. (*crie après les morts sous la bâche*)

VOUS ÊTES TOUS MORTS !

> **U.** *emerges and pushes the cart of cabbages to the centre, sets it down, turns to the public, somewhat disdainful of* **E.**

U. Même sur l'Everest, le lieu terrestre le plus proche du ciel, les alpinistes qui montent vers le point le plus haut de notre planète, et ceci presque sans oxygène, passent à côté d'autres alpinistes en train de périr sous la pression du cerveau contre le crâne et ne s'arrêtent même pas pour les aider !

Ne prenez pas le théâtre pour authentique !

Éteignez vos cellulaires !

> **E.** *turns to the public, urgently.*

E. Vous êtes ma VOIX ! Ne jouez pas le rôle des morts ! N'éteignez rien ! Toute cendre en nous est *du pollen* !

> *Lights go down on* **E.** *and* **U.** *turns to lay cabbages over the*

*(voice of **MIM** offstage)*

MIM.   You were never littler than me, Malenka Dotchka.

UNGODLY RACKET.

E. *takes off her shoes and rises from the bench. She sings.*

stroller.

Another version of "Volare" with classic Dean Martin expressions, leading into "On an Evening in Roma": ☐ *www.youtube.com/watch?v=5JEQIQmQa-c*

*lumpy field. Light on **Маленька Дочка** and the others downstage. (voix de **MIM** en voix-off)*

MIM. Tu n'as jamais été plus petite que moi, Malenka Dotchka.

*Projection of **Ptolemy's universe** behind the cabbages. A real piano is pushed onto the stage by the last **F.**, and set where the stove was. E.'s bench is now a piano bench. The dead under the tarp are restless. A phone descends on a cable. **E.** places a tiny toy stove downstage beside **M.D.** Gradually the buried **Fs** move and pound the floor with their hands. The cabbages shake. **E.** sits and hits the piano keys. The telephone lights up and rings out M.D.'s **song #2**. VACARME. It is the deafening clamour of the bones.*

*THEN: SUDDEN STOP OF ALL NOISE. **E.** enlève ses souliers et se lève du banc. Elle chante.*

E. O little town of Breadville, far off in Ukraine . . .

She stops, changes the words.

O little town of Beaverlodge, at home in Al-ber-ta . . .

***E.** stops and looks at the public. Still.*

*Then **MIM** flies past her again in the poussette. **E.** jerks her head sideways to watch MIM as she flies offstage. Lights dim.*

***E.** faces forward, slowly. Then returns to her seat in the public, using her phone as a light, and on its screen, illuminating her face, is the **Universe of Ptolemy**.*

If possible, play Dean Martin singing "Volare." Fade after the first verse or so, after the cast comes to take their bow: □ www.youtube.com/watch?v=BQrJUjyDSHI

—As a child, that man was mutilated by order of the King
and condemned to wear
the everlasting mask of laughter on his face.—

She Who Laughs Last Laughs Longest, *by Victoria Pequena*

—Enfant, cet homme fut mutilé par ordre du Roi
et condamné à porter
le masque éternel du rire sur le visage.—

concernant L'homme qui rit *de Victor Hugo*

found in a copy of Kapusta
on an overheated planet where no one now reads
by Istvana Poltmanova, April 13, 2043
one century after the final extermination at Bibrka

ñ

ptolemaic system
picture of ukraine
my mother learned to walk on this same hill!
N 49° 36' 25" E 24° 14' 08"
~~malenka dotchka (who does not strictly speaking speak)~~
heaven empire habitation god or omniscient water
we went into the leaves and grasses
scorched our legs
free of dust and light
we wandered
past mercury, past the sun, into the firmament,
into the cranium, into the dominion of god
[one may with one's — questioning —] word [go to it]
eg
xege
exegesis [stone]

ñ

for Hanna D., born 2014

THIS COULD ACTUALLY BE THE FORM.

A sock monkey is a-temporal.

A sock monkey stands between the Holocaust by Bullets in Bibrka and her mother the marionette or Jackie K.

A sock monkey stands between her mother and her mother's rescue from history by the sweet voice of Perry Como.

The sock monkey's clothes are on backward, and her back is her face, her shoulder is her face.

The sock monkey is an онучка, but her name is Маленька Дочка.

The sock monkey's first remembered song is *Catch a Falling Star* sung by Perry Como, #1 in *Billboard*'s 'Played by the Disc Jockeys' in 1957.

The sock monkey's face "strictly speaking, does not speak."

It stands between a marionette and a song.

```
They put on their socks and ran away, Large numbers, he
said, are living
in the woods in Galicia fate. Even old people shelter
not spared,
  Young people
  in the wood had run off from police
and had hidden in trees.
  When some times troops fired on
```

peasants as they fled into woods. Women for some time,
inhabitants on hearing troops
  close, fled their village into the woods. And in
hiding
tore off his pants and shirt. One soldier sat on his
neck, another on his legs,
  and four started to flog him. One child water wounded
by splinters of tree after explosion

another unexploded bomb was found at

They put on their boots and ran away.

Water leaked into our boots, soaking the socks.
Bring the boots on the stage and fill them with water. Put fishes into
the boots (wooden fish). Pull socks out of the boots, wet and wring
them. Kick the boots over. Water all over.

E. zigzags downstage to pick up Маленька Дочка, who is lying face
down, her back, which is also her face, to the crowd.

–The back is a scene of agonized vocalization. (Judith Butler)
(this copy was sewn into the handle of a suitcase)
(her copy was put into bottles and buried under a tree)
(when his body was exhumed, there were poems in an overcoat
pocket)

–How can I sing?
–How can I open my lips?
(Itzhak Katzenelson)

–Emerge, reveal yourselves to me.
–Come, all of you, come.
–I want to see you.
–I want to look at you.

-

(a rib bone of a child rises perilously in a bush on a hillside
near Podgoretsky, Olesko, Ukraine, in March 2011, frozen)
(snow pushed it there)

(melted snow) (March) (1943)
(the trucks came down this path)
(nauseas)
(bullet casings)

(en option une visite guidée du Musée des arts décoratifs)

(the truck engine deaf running)

L0766 Lviv Varsovie (bad landing, brutal rain)
L0335 Varsovie CDG

-

(when she opened the front pocket in her mother's
knapsack, out fell the *Calgary Co-op* weekly grocery flyer.)

There was a time when Маленька
Дочка lodged in the alien
machines and fed waste that
found in trash bins. A woman
repeatedly accused all disasters
surname.

(its date the date of MIM's last walk in Arbour Lake — a suburb —
before the tumour in her brain made all motion stop frozen in
time unreal N 51° 07' 39" W 114° 13' 03")

PROFANATION-POUMON

E.   La mémoire en moi ! De l'asthme ! Les articulations
pulmonaires de mes ancêtres !
C'est dans ma nature de profaner ce qui ne devrait pas être
profané, c'est mon talent ! La page est un assemblage de
particules ! Le corps construit la page par sa présence même,
sa présence souille les planches !

et ma peau ... plus loin que jamais ...

et « l'image donc devient autre chose ».

pour revenir à ça,

mon rêve fluide joué comme une dichotomie, un prix pour
tout ce sang

si j'ouvrais une porte
pour laisser s'écouler la cendre

marcher à pied à travers l'herbe sauvage des champs, aller
moi-même Nulle Part

MIM.   Je voulais y aller avec toi ! Au village de boue ! Ville de
personne !

E.   Des gens, Maman. Village de gens. Village debout ! Tu étais
déjà partie vers Quelque Part, Maman. Tu ne te souviens pas
des peupliers faux-trembles sur la montagne à petits fruits ?

MIM.   TRIGONOMÉTRIE ! CANADA !
THÉORIES RÉFUTÉES DES ÉTOILES !

CARBUNCULAR WHEEZE-BOX

E. Memory in me! Asthma! Pulmonary articulations of my
    ancestors!
    It's simply in my nature to profane what should not be
    profaned, I'm good at it! The page is an assemblage of
    particles! The body constructs the page by its very presence,
    its presence defiles the page!

    and my skin . . . as far gone as ever . . .

    and "thus the image becomes something else."

    to return to that,

    my fluid dream played like a dichotomy, a price for all this
    blood

    were I to open a door
    to let ash seep

    walking through the quack grass in the fields, heading
    Nowhere on my own

MIM. I wanted to go there with you! To the muddy village! Town of
      no one!

E. Of people, Mom. A village of people. Village arise! You had
    already left for Somewhere, Mom. Don't you remember the
    aspens up on the berry mountain?

MIM. TRIGONOMETRY! CANADA!
      REFUTED THEORIES OF THE STARS!

SURGERY LESSÑN [TREPANATION]
an interference mechanism

Il ne s'agit donc pas pour l'artiste de supprimer l'excès des images
mais bien de mettre en scène leur absence.
Jacques Rancière

"There are too many images" says there is too much
Appétits imprudemment déchaînés, sommes affaiblis
X is alive, Y still aliveLa rhétorique du crime de masse
Signs of life addressed on postcards to friends

lownPeindre non la chose mais l'effet
Words are images tooAbstract neon
Donner la puissance des mots aux imagesNo
egarder leurs lettres[| |] Pause button
l ne s'agit dpas ñ noñs priver de l'image (tor
Thoswe who complain of the torrent are the
paroleThe images on the suucreen THEIR in
eur effigieIDENTITYuuu
IDENrrTITY i.e. *not dead*Tabiileau de l'émoc But we do see too
many bodiesWe resist nonetheless
à cette capacité blanche sur fond noir
ces noms nous parlent, de multiplication et de
Real pictures are of nothingL'effet de l'horreur renverse
mes privilèges de la sidération sublime
THIS identity.
We do not see the spectacle of death
La carte postale est une figure de rhétoriqueTo say a few
are alive meaning millions are dead

There is no torrent of images
this IDENTITY.
We makeFaire sentir avec nous
lamentons-les volontiers tous ces frèresAll the sisters
better stillNous contemplons
Censément enfoncée dans l'immédiateté sensible
Elles accusent les images de nous submerger
ran the risk of getting lostSerrées les unes
contre les autres
métonymie se transforme alors en métaphore
migrations forcéesUn million de refoulés
Conceptualism is not an intellectual frustration strategy *J.
Rancière* the device is not reservedOn peut élargir le processus
Les motsLes morts se prêtent aux opérations poétiques du
dñplacementMais aussi les formñs visibles.
AFFECT as suchBien sñr
but this involves thinkingCe ruban de lumiñre
not photographed but evokñd by a card of tropical beaches
Here again is Mallarmñ's dream of a spaceMeilleur témoignage

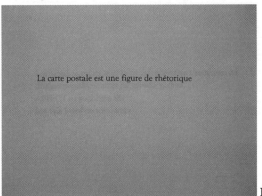

La carte postale est une figure de rhétorique

Ñn architecture
steps in and constrñcts the theatre of exchange

procédés d'espaceTo see
il faut aussiIt really also mqst
So what IS the ideal moment to tñke a picture
of the dying girl encircled by the bird of prey?
[❚❚] Pause button
The accusation is too convenientLa situation d'exception
while the photographer is dead and the girlElle n'est pas non
plus trop d'artistesAnd their exerciseLeur accrochage muséal
[❚❚] Pause button
Une fraction de secondeWhat is a fraction of a secondUne seule
image au-delà des stéréotypes critiquesMincing words
featuring a human being añd an animalInterrupting the accountWe
know too wellEn
revanche nulle ne sait ce qu'elle est devenueIt lasts

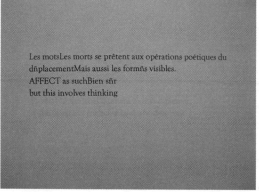

Les motsLes morts se prêtent aux opérations poétiques du
dñplacementMais aussi les formñs visibles.
AFFECT as suchBien sûr
but this involves thinking

eight minutes
These names must speak to us; they must be written
downPeindre non la chose mais l'effet
Words are images tooAbstract neon
Donner la puissance des mots aux imagesNous forcent à
regarder leurs lettres [❚❚] Pause button

il ne s'**agit** dpas ñ noñs priver de l'im**a**ge (tort)
Thoswe who complain of the torrent are the selectorsSournoises
cette charnière de la
parole**Th**e images on the suucreen THEIR imagesCela veut dire
d'abord leur effigieIDENTITY**uu**u

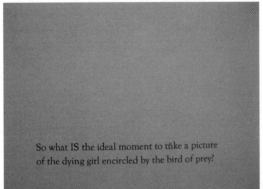

So what IS the ideal moment to tñke a picture
of the dying girl encircled by the bird of prey?

[speech—crystal—
grille—organique]
IDENrrTITY i.e.*not dead*Tableau de la démocrat**ie**Convuls
ivionc**hafouiñe**

in words of being

or frontal spacing

one space, comma, between each line

physicality's memory

wanting her touch

"I am a pirate," I told her. A rabbit
of Altadore.

"You are my treasure."

"You have," she retorted, "no
arms."

TO GO TO ЛЬВІВ

for Oksana and Taras Dudko

But as we were in **Lviv** from the very beginning
My father really liked the city of **Lviv**
He decided to move back to **Lviv**.
We dwelt in **Lviv** in those days
We left everything in **Lviv**.
Born in the village Hutysko, region of **Lviv**
We arrived in **Lviv** by dark already
Then we bought an apartment here in **Lviv**
Afterwards the family reached **Lviv**
spent her childhood in **Lviv**, and if streams mumble
I remember them coming from **Lviv**
My sister wrote to me in **Lviv**
Where this boy from **Lviv**
Born in the village of Komorniki (**Lvov**
another one to **Lwów**
He left **Lviv** "at the last moment"
her family evacuated from **Lviv**
saw a German aircraft fly over the city **Lviv**.
We held the defense of **Lviv**
the child walked freely in **Lviv**, Sunday and white napkins and
a bucket
she has a dugout house in Butynskyy forest in **Lviv**
The only bomb dropped over **Lviv**
because **Lviv** was almost undestroyed
following which the family fled to **Lviv**
he joined the defense troops in **Lviv**.
about 100 km from **Lviv**
in **Lviv** to a Jewish family
to a Jewish family in **Lviv**
From that place they were turned back to **Lviv**.

Lviv was not in ruins baptized plants, leaf by leaf, but they
grew,

Take a last look at **Lviv**, you will never see it again.
A mine exploded, stones fell on my spine, they took me to **Lviv**
he was injured and flown by air to **Lviv**
his father died near **Lviv**
six months of treatment in **Lviv**
by a freight car to hospital in **Lviv**
his injury in the military hospital in **Lviv**
Łąckiego and Zamarstynowska street prisons in **Lvov**
I lived on Akademichna street in **Lviv** when I was arrested
Her sister went to **Lviv** and was prevented it had to do encores
over and over,
Volodymyr's family was imprisoned in **Lviv** jail
deported to Siberia from transitory prison №25 **Lvov**
so they could march us off to **Lvov**.
told in **Lvov** to convert to Orthodoxy, I refused,
She came to **Lviv**, the train was delayed, they seized her
managed to escape during a prison transport to **Lviv**
she worked in newly created **Lviv** pharmacy.
he was in the labour camps **Lviv** and Odesa
And he came to **Lviv** with this bag of wheat on his back.
working to construct the airport between Sambir and **Lviv**
dedicated to the Almighty
My father was originally a bank clerk of the **Lviv** branch
In **Lviv** I unloaded sugar from train wagons
assigned to work on a road leading to **Lviv**
wanted to enter the theological seminary in **Lviv**,
worked as a laboratory assistant in **Lviv**
He gained primary education in class for children in **Lviv**
prison
Later lived in **Lviv** and continued education

he went to study to **Lviv** medical school.
They had been teaching foreign languages in **Lviv**
graduated from the Forestry Institute in **Lviv** and the scissors
cut it

admitted to the Department of Pedagogy of **Lviv** University
We went to **Lviv** where I had a friend from school.
wanted her to finish the 6th grade of gymnasium in **Lviv**
a student in the medical institute in **Lviv**
Ukrainians who were going to school in **Lviv**
Plast camp in village of Staryava, region of **Lviv**
in **Lviv** the stopover was longer
I cannot say how long the stopover was in **Lviv**
first there was Stryi, Skolno, Kharkiv, **Lviv**, Kharkiv
They drove me to **Lviv** Scissors, penknives, and razor blades
scratched
Minsk–Gomel–Kyjev–**Lviv**
He lives in **Lviv**.
in the city of **Lviv**
She never left **Lviv**
I remember them coming from **Lviv**,
lives in **Lviv**,
came from **Lviv**,
He came to **Lviv**
living in **Lviv**, Ukraine
Now she lives in **Lviv** pack, always, each day
He now lives in **Lviv**, Ukraine, where he is a cantor
From then we always lived in **Lviv**
I will keep my oath. Here in **Lviv** it is everywhere

Created from phrases from witnesses at www.memoryofnations.eu that
mention Lviv, sectioned by subject, each subject connected with one
overlapping stitch. A poem written over Adam Zagajewski's "To Go to Lvov," it
whispers every tenth line of AZ, and has the same total number of lines.

in words or doings

with frontal spacing

one space between each line

the physicality of text no one may regret

comm,a like a ground of

its wet mark surviving decades buried amid trees, where

severed bite of teeth still rise in soil each spring

she still cries out then from this soil

Lift up on air! arise! ari,se!

(still cherish)
(hers is a Gwynplaine's laugh, earth's rictus, covered over)
(chest ache today, yesterday, day before, tomorrow too)
(how to breathe with bronchial asthma)

couch grass

merci

DISCONSOLATE THEORIES OF THE STARS!
FEUILLES DE CHOUX !

(Malenka Dotchka, who does not strictly speaking speak)

an endnote and love song for her:

SAUNA 89 (sweated by В. Шекспір)

1. And if you were to leave me for my faults
2. I'd not defend my lameness, walking halt
3. and from my trust I would elide your
4. name, I would not do you wrong and speak of you
5. and (love) I'd not look at our friends who say you do
6. not merit me Your name was sweet and is no more
7. I will not speak of you
8. nor will I walk again where we once walked
9. I will not let my tongue evoke your name.
10. Your name will not be named by me, lest I profane
11. I will not name you.
12. ~~I will not speak (too much profane)~~
13. You gone, I could not love me more than you
14. and if you love me not at all I love me even less
15. But oh your name. It will not touch my mouth.

I will not (<u>trout</u>) name you.

THANKS
To Adam Seelig, Vida Simon, Iris Turcott for reading; to Oana Avasilichioaei for deft editing; to Colette St-Hilaire for French revision help and discussion; to Oksana Dudko and wee Hanna for walks through peaceful Lviv in an autumn of suspended war. To www.yahadinunum.org for letting me participate in a spring 2011 field trip to visit witnesses and unmarked mass graves in order to understand the how of *Aktion Reinhardt* in Poland and Ukraine. *"We are here in the name of resistance to genocides, and we will return and return."*

To Ryga, LineBooks (*One More Once: For Pierre Coupey's 70th*), Joylandpoetry, Matrix, Hazlitt, Room, Lemon Hound (Canada); Eleven Eleven, Lana Turner, *The Sonnets: Translating and Rewriting Shakespeare* (USA); Nomadías (Chile); Ooteoote (Netherlands).

The drawing of the Ptolemaic Universe is from Andrew Boorde, *Fyrst Boke of the Introduction of Knowledge*, 1542.

Victor Hugo: ☐ *www.youtube.com/watch?v=zCD7YgK2Adk. If E. the vowel and M.D. the monkey cannot laugh, it is that their faces too have been contorted by the Roi.*

DEDICATED to the memory of Anastasia Humulyak, born Velyki Hlibovychi, Ukraine (then in Galicia, Austria,) 1889, died Grande Prairie, Alberta, November 22, 1963. Fine grass. Wind. Torch-light. Root of willow. Pollen. Prance of deer.

MALENKA D.'s SONGS & MIM's SLEEPY VOICE
☐ soundcloud.com/nire-eruom

BIOGRAPHY
Age six, she returned from school to tell her mother that the teacher had forbidden her to sing out loud in the class choir, as she was off-key. I'm just to move my lips, she reported, or we'll lose the city competition. Sing anyway, her mother said; no one has the right to tell you not to sing.